SOULISTRY

– *Artistry of the Soul*

Creative Ways to Nurture Your Spirituality

Other books by the author:
Disturbed by God: A Journey of Spiritual Discovery
ISBN 1-55126-153-7
Maffin, June Mack
Spiritual autobiography

Spiritual life – Anglicans
Now available as an e-book:
http://www.soulistry.com/books/dbg
BV4011.6.M3   1996   248.4   C96-930164-2

SOULISTRY
– *Artistry of the Soul*

Creative Ways to Nurture Your Spirituality

June Mack Maffin

Hampshire, England
Cleveland, Ohio

First published by Circle Books, 2011
Circle-Books is an imprint of John Hunt Publishing Ltd., Laurel House, Station Approach,
Alresford, Hants, SO24 9JH, UK
office1@o-books.net
www.o-books.com

For distributor details and how to order please visit the 'Ordering' section on our website.

Text copyright: June Mack Maffin 2010

ISBN: 978 1 84694 615 8

A CIP catalogue record for this book is available from the British Library.

Design: Stuart Davies

Printed in the UK by CPI Antony Rowe
Printed in the USA by Offset Paperback Mfrs, Inc

We operate a distinctive and ethical publishing philosophy in all areas
of our business, from our global network of authors to production
and worldwide distribution.

Contents

Acknowledgements

Special appreciation to Authors (their Executors/Trust
companies/record labels/agents) who graciously gave
permission to use their words as Soulistry Journal Prompts
and to
Harlene Walker
Timothy Staveteig
Linda Maloney
and AWCCer's around the globe
who caught the vision for this book.

Dedication

To those who have brought me
to
through
and beyond the mountains
valleys, lessons
experiences, sufferings
endings
and new beginnings of life
I offer my humble thanks.

By word, action and example
they have taught me
what it is to hope
rejoice, play,
trust, accept, love
forgive, give thanks
celebrate and delight in
the gift of each day.

To my parents, Eddie and Joy Mack
now deceased, but who are always with me
To my siblings, Gerry Mack and Fran Talbot
who love and support from afar
To my son, Tod Maffin
who has always made me proud to be his mother
and who courageously lives day by day
with tenacity and determination
And to my husband, Hans van der Werff
whose love brings joy to my life in so many ways
I dedicate this book with thanksgiving and much love.

*Soulistry is a coined word (combining two words: soul and artistry) created by the author and Tod Maffin www.todmaffin.com

Preface

How to Get the Most out of this Book

To get the most out of this book, readers are encouraged to reflect on the Soulistry Journal Prompts and journal their responses to the Soul-Questions. For some, this may be a simple matter because journaling is something you've done before and are comfortable doing. For others, it may be daunting because you've never journaled and don't know how to begin. So, how to begin?

> **Step One**: *Get a Journal. It can simply be blank pages of paper you've put into a binder or duotang folder. It could be a Journal you've purchased - art supply stores, book stores, card shops and pharmacies often carry journals. Or, it could be something you've made. Near the end of this book in the Appendices section, you'll find directions for making a Soulistry Journal. It's easy to do and who knows, it just may take you on an artistic journey into the wonderful (wonder-filled) world of journal and book making.*
>
> **Step Two**: *Once you've got your Journal, put your name in it. You've now begun journaling.*
>
> **Step Three**: *As you move through the Journal Prompts (quotations) and their Soul-Questions, find one that "speaks" to you. The order isn't important – begin wherever you want to begin. Write the quotation in your Soulistry Journal, add the first question and write your response. Then the second question and write your response to that, following this process with each Soulistry Journal Prompt. Writing a date at the top of the page as you complete the Soul-Questions can encourage you on your spiritual journey of self-awareness, self-acceptance and self-confidence.*

Journal writings are meant to be personal conversations - with yourself/with yourself and God. Writing your responses to the

Soul-Questions can clarify what you believe/think about certain relationships, issues, life, yourself. This is your opportunity to know yourself more deeply and to make time to listen, to think, to pray, to meditate about what you believe – really believe. You may find that your responses to the Soul-Questions raise additional questions and if so, record those questions in your Soulistry Journal for consideration at a later time.

In the process of responding to the Soulistry Soul-Questions, anticipate a deepening of spiritual awareness as you confront times in your life that had moments of hope, joy, peace, celebration and moments when you were fragile and in the midst of pain, loneliness, fear, suffering, questioning, anxiety, doubt.

Step Four: *Consider creating a new Soulistry Journal and repeating the above steps at significant moments of your life - birth of a child, loss of a pet, at crossroad-ages, ending of a relationship, becoming a senior citizen, loss of a job, death of a loved one, time of critical illness. These can become a personal record of your thoughts, feelings and opinions at specific times in your life. They can help you see where you've changed and how you've matured. And they can point to areas you might want to work on for further self-growth and spiritual enrichment.*

An aside: Generally, journal entries are personal and not intended to be shared with others. However, it might be helpful to seek the input and guidance of another. A pastoral counselor, soul friend/spiritual director is trained in listening skills and can assist you in understanding the holiness that lies in the ordinary – those daily tasks, mundane encounters, simple everyday moments of life. To learn more about spiritual direction/soul friendship in general and get assistance in particular for a spiritual director/soul friend in your geographical area, contact Spiritual Directors International www.sdiworld.org

Prologue

Questions. Many are asking them these days. The anxiety produced by the seemingly never-ending economic woes, terrorism, global oil crisis, environmental issues, our own personal/medical crises and more seem to be creating a global atmosphere of fear, anxiety, loneliness and alienation of spirit. Connection with Spirit is tenuous for many.

And yet ... and yet. And yet there is a growing indefinable awareness of the importance of balance in people's lives (physically, intellectually, spiritually, emotionally) and that being spiritual is a vital component of one's personhood.

Regardless of educational background, work experience, age, race, language, gender, religion or cultural upbringing, our spiritual nature calls forth questions - questions about the meaning of life: *"Who am I?"* *"Why is there suffering in the world?"* *"Does God exist?"* *"What is my purpose?"* *"What happens after I die?"* *"Why has this illness / accident happened to my loved one/friend?"*

In spite of all that can seem negative, disheartening, discouraging, sad, confusing, evil, unjust, fearful etc. in one's personal life and in the world, inner peace, abundant joy and a sense of direction and purpose is possible as soul-space is created.

But, how can that be done? Where will we find the time to squeeze yet another 'something' into our already hectic lives? There are many who are paying others to 'give them the answer' to happiness, peace, financial security, relationship and work stability in the context of weekend conferences and workshops. But is that necessary? Can we not find those answers to our questions within ourselves?

Questions and more questions. They're not necessarily religious or unusual questions. They are questions that need soul-space. Soul-Questions.

Perhaps the Greeks can help us out. They used two words to explain the different dimensions of time - καιρός and χρόνος – 'kairos' and 'chronos'.

Chronos time is the time spent going to work, school or involvement with volunteer activities. It's those pedantic, clock-watching moments of every day when we're doing the laundry, picking up the groceries, putting out the garbage, taking the children to their after-school activities, washing the dishes. We're usually very good when it comes to the chronos of our lives.

Kairos is more elusive. It's those treasured moments when we make time to simply "be"; when we get in touch with our true selves; when we see the miracles about us and know beyond all knowing from an intellectual point of view that there is something (SomeOne – however we name that Essence) greater than ourselves. Kairos is soul-space time.

Kairos moments happen when we are sitting by the bedside of a sick child/aged parent quietly reading to them ... holding a newborn baby ... watching a caterpillar burst into a beautiful butterfly ... noting the formation of clouds in the sky ... being reassured by the gentle purring of a cat or nuzzling of a dog ... hearing a piece of music that sends shivers up our spine ... reading a portion of scripture we've read countless times before and having it leap from the page with a meaning we'd never before encountered ... receiving and giving a hug ... having a smile returned by a stranger ... enjoying a moment of prayer in the tub, church pew, favorite chair, shower ... being aware of the gift of our breath unassisted by mechanical means ... holding the hand of someone who is dying ... sitting in silence before the ocean or fireplace and hearing affirmation that you were called into being and are deeply loved ... slowly eating a meal, truly tasting and appreciating its sight and taste ... receiving a gift from another who, for no reason, chose to bless your day by giving you a present of time or material possession ... being aware of tears gently flowing down our cheeks as we watch a movie or read a book that deeply touches us ... having fun in the kitchen making a casserole or cookies you'll share with another ... gasping at the rainbow that arcs across the horizon ... walking through a cemetery and being aware of the frailty and fragility of life and its temporal nature... laughing a deep, from-the-belly-kind-of-laugh.

So often we ignore the kairos times in our lives and don't make time to 'smell the flowers.'

How often do we experience the healing and compassionate presence in another's smile, touch, phone call, visit, letter, embrace, handshake, eye contact, tears as kairos? When are silence and solitude experienced as 'gift'?

There is difficulty seeing beyond the immediate moment to a global connectedness. Rarely is the holy acknowledged in and through the laughter and smile of a child ... the brilliant colors of a peacock's tail ... the industriousness of an ant ... the grace of a butterfly ... the agility of a gymnast ... the speed of cyber-space communication ... the unconditional love of a pet ... the gentleness of lovers ... the subtle fragrance of a rose ... the miracle of birth ... the genius of design in a spider's web ... the time taken to simply 'be'.

Over the years, I have come to experience spiritual growth as I ask Soul-Questions of myself: *"How can I grow more fully into my humanity?" "How can I continue my journey of 'becoming' and reach my full potential?" "How can I deepen my awareness of the presence of the holy around me?" "How can I fully embrace life?" "How can I recognize and celebrate my inner wisdom?"* For me, spirituality is an exploration of the deep mysteries of life which can happen anywhere and anytime - in nature, in moments of confusion, at times of silence, in interpersonal relationships, during meditation, among community, in solitude, at a point of crisis, at peace, in worship, in sickness, during prayer, at times of health and even during times of doubt and questioning.

And that brings me to the reason for this book.

I have had the rare and humbling privilege of accompanying people on their spiritual journey for several decades. In that time, I have come to appreciate the wisdom found in the words of others. So it was that quotations found their way into my card file and Soul-Questions around those quotations began to formulate for sojourners.

As they journaled their responses to the Soul-Questions, a poignant understanding of who they were becoming, began to evolve. The quotations and Soul-Questions sparked a thought, a memory, an opinion, a question, challenging them to dig within more deeply.

An often-quoted proverb by Thomas Jefferson goes something like this: Don't put off to tomorrow what you can do today. While those words are usually addressed to the chronos moments of our lives, it is my hope that this book of Soulistry Journal Prompts and Soul-Questions will encourage you to connect more intimately with your spirituality; reflect on the "kairos" moments of your life; honor your personal story through the wisdom of words through the ages; and offer new ways to nurture your spirit. Before you know it, the time you take to simply "be" will become the catalyst and conduit for that precious balance you so genuinely seek to emerge.

By the way, there is no need to rush through the Soulistry Journal Prompts (quotations) – or the Soul-Questions. Allow kairos to be your companion. Take time – make time ... over a period of days, weeks, months or even years.

Each time you are ready to receive a Soulistry Journal Prompt and its accompanying Soul-Questions, find a comfortable chair, perhaps a hot cup of tea on the table beside you, a beloved pet at your feet, quiet music in the background.

This is your time. So, take a deep breath and inhale Spirit (God, Presence, Source, Holy Other, Creator, Higher Power, G_d) who seeks to bring wholeness, clarity, peace and joy as you continue your journey of self-discovery.

As you look at the world around you ... as you consider the decisions that must be made ... as you become aware of the people you meet ... as you enter into situations you encounter ... and as you experience the moments of crisis and moments of joy, may you come to realize that all life is holy and that in the ordinariness of life, there is true holiness.

May this book with its Soul-Questions nurture your spirituality. May it encourage your journey of self-discovery as you come to a deeper understanding of who you are. And may your Soulistry Journal provide a precious and unique window to your soul. Shalom. Blessings. Namaste.

June

soulistry@gmail.com
www.soulistry.com

Soulistry Journal Prompts and Soul-Questions

Gift

Soulistry Journal Prompt ... Denis Brown

Everybody has a gift. Your job is to find it, love it, nourish it and give it space to grow. It's not too late for anyone to commit to making space for their own nature to blossom.

Used by permission.

Soulistry Soul-Questions

* What is your understanding of the word *"gift"* in the above context?
* Have you yet determined the nature of your gift? What is it?
* How can you *"find"* your gift? *"love"* this gift? *"nourish"* your gift?
* How can you *"give it space to grow"*?
* How much *"space"* do you need in your life (time-wise, physically, etc,) for your gift to grow?
* How can you make *"space"* in your life for your *"nature to blossom"*?
* What other gifts have you not yet opened - artistic gifts, communication gifts, administrative gifts, helping gifts, leadership gifts, teaching gifts, etc.?
* How might you explore these gifts?

Nothing You Can Do

Soulistry Journal Prompt ... Desmond Tutu

There is nothing you can do that will make God love you more. There is nothing you can do that will make God love you less.

Used by permission

Soulistry Soul-Questions

* Do you believe that God (Creator, Holy Other, Higher Power, Spirit, Holy One) loves you? If so, is that love conditional or unconditional?
* If that love is conditional, on what is it conditional?
* Can you recall instances when you tried to do something to *"make God love you more"*? Reflect on those moments in your Soulistry Journal.
* Do you think there are **levels** of the Creator's love? **Situations** where God loves more? **People** who are loved more by the Creator? **Religions** God loves more? **Countries** loved more by the Creator? If so, journal your thoughts about those situations.
* Are there instances in your life when you have experienced unconditional love? Create space in your day so you can make time to reflect on those moments.
* If you do not believe that you are loved unconditionally, can you identify what has contributed to have you come to this conclusion?
* If *"there is nothing more you can do to make God love you more than you are already loved,"* what motivates your life?
* If *"there is nothing you can do that will make God love you less,"* what can you do to bring about a deeper awareness of the Creator's love and presence in the moments of self-doubt, anxiety, sinfulness, shame, guilt etc.?

The Well Within

Soulistry Journal Prompt ... Thich Nhat Hanh

The well is within us. If we dig deeply in the present moment, the water will spring forth.

Soulistry Soul-Questions

* What do you think the author means by *"the well is within"*?
* How have you dug *"deeply in the present moment"* in your life?
* What growth/learning/self-discoveries resulted from such reflection?
* How might you begin to *"dig deeply in the present moment"*?
* Are there things in your past or evident in this present time that are preventing you from looking at the well within you? If so, name/journal them/talk them over with a counselor/spiritual director/soul friend so these things no longer have power over you, restricting your ongoing tapping of the well-within.
* What *"water"* do you hope *"will spring forth"* from such self-examination?

A Spirituality of Play

Soulistry Journal Prompt ... Margaret Guenther

When we play, we also celebrate holy uselessness. Like the calf frolicking in the meadow, we need no pretense or excuses. Work is productive; play, in its disinterestedness and self-forgetting, can be fruitful. When we forget to play, we've forgotten the joy of creation.

Used by permission.

Soulistry Soul-Questions

* How might a spirituality of play become cultivated in society and our educational systems so that children and youth develop into adults whose lives are filled with laughter, joy and hope?

* The English word 'silly' comes from the Greek word 'selig' meaning blessed. How can you more fully develop such a blessed (holy) state in your life?

* Various faith traditions (i.e. Hasidic and Christian story-tellers; Zen masters; Taoist sages; Hindus who speak of the creation of the universe as the **play** of God, not the **work** of God) encourage people not to take themselves too seriously. Are you someone who finds it easy to play – to be silly? Reflect on what/who has been instrumental in your life to allow this playfulness to be part of your personhood or who/what has blocked it.

* Literature, the arts, even our holidays (holy-days) remind us of the importance of playing, of giving ourselves permission to take time to be silly and foolish i.e. 15th century Russian artists often featured the yurodivy, a kind of 'holy fool' in their paintings ... April Fool's Day is a day for laughing, for playing gentle jokes and tricking friends ... on the last day of the Huli Festival in India, people delight in sending friends on impossible errands such as

finding a stick with only one end. In your Soulistry Journal, reflect on the moments in your adult life when you have been playful to the point of silliness. Describe:
- the situation
- who was with you
- your thoughts and feelings at the time and afterwards
* Playing can be a sacred activity, as sacred an activity as are silence, solemnity and prayer. Reflect on your understanding and belief about a spirituality of play and how it can nurture your spirit.
* How can you remember *"the joy of creation"* in your playing this week?

Questions That Speak

Soulistry Journal Prompt ... Chinese Proverb
Those who ask questions may be fools for five minutes; but those who do not ask remain fools forever.

Soulistry Soul-Questions
* What questions do you have about
  - life
  - yourself
  - the world
  - love
  - forgiveness
  - eternity
  - death?
* It's been said that questions have more importance than answers. What questions have been more important to you than the answers?
* What questions have prompted (spoken to) you on your spiritual journey?
* In your Soulistry Journal, reflect on one of those questions. Why was this particular question more important than the answer?
* Have there been questions about individuals/situations /finances/values/background that you did not ask and wish you had? In your Soulistry Journal, reflect on those questions and how you might move beyond whatever blocked you in those circumstances.

Secret of the Spiritual Life

Soulistry Journal Prompt ... Gerald Heard

The whole secret of the spiritual life is just this painful struggle to come awake, to become really conscious.

The Creed of Christ (Eugene: Wipf and Stock Publishers, 2008, pp.79-80).

Used by permission.

Soulistry Soul-Questions

* What does *"to come awake, to become really conscious"* mean for you?
* Have you experienced your life, your spiritual journey as *"struggle"* - as *"painful"*?
* If so, how?
* How would you describe your *"spiritual life"* today?
* If you could have described your spiritual life a year ago, how might you have described it?
* Where would you like to see your *"spiritual life"* in a year?
* What/who might help you achieve these goals?

Doing Good

Soulistry Journal Prompt ... John Wesley

Do all the good you can, by all the means you can, in all the ways you can, in all the places you can, at all the times you can, to all the people you can, as long as ever you can.

Soulistry Soul-Questions

* In Wesley's context, what does *"good"* mean to you?
* Reflect and journal about moments in your life when you did *"all the good"* you could.
* Journal about the times when the good you did was by *"all the means"* you had at the time.
* Reflect on the rest of Wesley's words. Was the *"good"* done in *"all the ways ... all the places ... at all the times ... to all the people"* you could?
* How might you adopt Wesley's holy-living lifestyle into your life?

Mystery

Soulistry Journal Prompt ... Martin Buber

Real faith means holding ourselves open to the unconditional mystery which we encounter in every sphere of our life.

Soulistry Soul-Questions

* What does the word *"mystery"* mean to you?
* Is mystery encountered *"in every sphere"* of your life? If so, reflect on this in your Soulistry Journal.
* If mystery is not encountered in such a way, journal how you might 'hold yourself open' to mystery in your life
  - artistically
  - relationally
  - spiritually
  - environmentally
  - creatively
  - politically
  - economically

The Mark of Wisdom

Soulistry Journal Prompt ... Ralph Waldo Emerson

The invariable mark of wisdom is to see the miraculous in the common.

Soulistry Soul-Questions

* What was your response as you reflected on Frost's three words expressing what he had learned about life: *"It goes on"*?

* If you could add words to Emerson's three words to expand on the concept that life *"goes on"*, what would those words be?

* Have there been moments in your life when you've experienced life as anything but 'going-on' ... when it was stagnant, blocked or seemed to move backwards? Reflect on one of these times in your Soulistry Journal.

* Were you able to recognize the stagnancy, blockage, backward-moving action as it was happening, shortly afterwards, much later? Reflect on those moments of recognition in your Soulistry Journal.

* Were you able to recognize these on your own or was another involved in helping you recognize where you were? Reflect on this person (these persons) and journal about your experience and their involvement.

* How did (and do) you get past the stagnancy, the blockage so that life *"goes on"* for you?

Faith

Soulistry Journal Prompt ... Patrick Overton

When you walk to the edge of all the light you have
and take that first step into the darkness of the unknown,
you must believe that one of two things will happen:
  There will be something solid for you to stand upon,
  or, you will be taught how to fly.

Used by permission © Patrick Overton The Leaning Tree, 1975

Rebuilding the Front Porch of America, 1997

Soulistry Soul-Questions

* Reflect on a time in your life when you came *"to the edge of all the light"* you knew and were *"about to step off into the darkness of the unknown."* What happened?
* Were you aware that either *"there will be something solid to stand on"* or *"you will be taught to fly"* at the time? Which was it for you?
* What led to that awareness?
* Spend time with your Soulistry Journal describing the *"something solid"* or what the 'flying' was about in this particular moment.
* How would you describe what the word *"faith"* means to you?

Happiness

Soulistry Journal Prompt ... Chinese Proverb

If you want happiness for an hour, take a nap. If you want happiness for a day, go fishing. If you want happiness for a lifetime, help someone else.

Soulistry Soul-Questions

* Do 'being happy' and 'being joyful' have the same meaning for you?
* If not, what is the difference?
* What contributes to your happiness?
* In your Soulistry Journal, reflect on a time in your life when you were happy. What was the occasion/circumstance? How did you feel?
* How can helping another bring happiness to the helper?
* What can you do to *"help someone else"* on a regular basis?
* Are there individuals, or community/environmental /political/religious organizations you might help? Journal who they might be and how you might be able to offer to help them.

What is Spirituality

Soulistry Journal Prompt ... Dan Wakefield

Spirituality emerges in care for family, friends and fellow human beings, in the passion for learning and perfecting one's craft, for enjoying and appreciating the commonplace gifts of everyday experience and finding in them the inspiration for living more fully.

Used by permission.

Soulistry Soul-Questions

* What resonated within you when you read Wakefield's definition of spirituality? What did not?
* Does religion play a part in your understanding of spirituality? If so, how?
* How have you cared for *"friends and fellow human beings"*?
* How have you been passionate *"for learning and perfecting"*?
  - your life
  - your art
  - your studies
  - your craft
  - your work
* If you have enjoyed and appreciated *"the commonplace gifts of everyday experience"* and found in them *"the inspiration for living more fully"*, what have you done to be able to do so?
* Would you define yourself primarily as a religious or spiritual person? How so?
* What do you see to be the difference between religion and spirituality?
* What factors entered into your self-definition as primarily religious or spiritual?

Risking Frustration

Soulistry Journal Prompt ... Thomas Merton

To hope is to risk frustration. Therefore, make up your mind to risk frustration.

Used by permission of New Directions Publishing.

Soulistry Soul-Questions

* When have you *"risked frustration"* in order to hope and live a better, more spiritually/emotionally/physically /intellectually/relationally/environmentally/economically fulfilling life?

* Take some time to reflect on the moments when you didn't *"risk frustration"*. What blocked your ability to do so?

* Is there a pattern that emerges in your ability to *"risk frustration"*?

* What can you do to *"make up your mind to risk frustration"* so that hope can re-enter your life the next time life hits you with a bitter pill to swallow, an unfair situation, an injustice?

The Web Of Life

Soulistry Journal Prompt ... traditionally attributed to Chief Seattle

Humankind has not woven the web of life. We are but one thread within it. Whatever we do to the web, we do to ourselves. All things are bound together. All things connect.

Soulistry Soul-Questions

* Reflect on the *"web of life"* metaphor. How do you see yourself as *"but one thread within"* the web of life?
* How might *"whatever we do to the web* (of life), *we do to ourselves"* become fulfilled?
* In your Soulistry Journal, reflect on a recent action that you have taken - or not taken. How might that action or lack of action affected others ... family, friends, strangers, enemies, neighbors?
* Reflect on your connection with the *"web of life"* vis-à-vis stewardship of the earth ... conservation of water/electricity, recycling, 'natural' versus synthetic products, choice of vehicle, etc. in your Soulistry Journal. What impact might your action/lack of action in these areas have on your life - your loved ones - the next/subsequent generations?
* Reflect on the statement: *"all things are bound together ... all things connect"*. How are you/humankind connected to the earth, the seas and oceans, the animals, the plants, your neighbors?
* Who are your neighbors?
* If your understanding of neighbor includes those in distant lands, those you have never met, those who have a different (or no) understanding of a Higher Power God/the Creator, those who are not-yet-born ... does that

understanding affect your belief about
- other religions
- abortion
- same-sex blessings/marriages,
- euthanasia,
- capital punishment?
* If so, journal how it does in each instance.

Peace Within

Soulistry Journal Prompt ... Jill Jackson

Let there be peace on earth, and let it begin with me.
Let there be peace on earth, the peace that was meant to be.
With God our Creator, family all are we.
{alternate sentence "With Earth as our Mother, her children all are we:}
Let us walk with each other, in perfect harmony.
Let peace begin with me, let this be the moment now.
With every step I take, let this be my solemn vow:
to take each moment and live each moment in peace eternally.
Let there be peace on earth, and let it begin with me.

Soulistry Soul-Questions

* How would you define *"peace"*?
* Would your definition change if the question had been worded "how would you define **world** peace?"
* Would your definition change if the question had been worded inner peace"? If so, reflect on each of these in your Soulistry Journal.
* In your Soulistry Journal, reflect on where you are in your life vis-à-vis peace in relation to your
  - family
  - job
  - health
  - finances
  - relationships
  - beliefs
* How can you find peace within yourself?
* How might you be a bearer of peace in today's world?
* As you reflect on Jill Jackson's lyrics, how might people

"walk with each other in perfect harmony"?

* Are you ready to make a *"solemn vow: to take each moment and live each moment in peace"*?

* What do you need to do to make this vow become reality?

Soul-Stars

Soulistry Journal Prompt ... Pamela Vaull Starr

Reach high, for stars lie hidden in your soul. Dream deep, for every dream precedes the goal.

Soulistry Soul-Questions

* What dreams do you have that are unfulfilled goals?
* What stars *"lie hidden in your soul"*?
* How can you *"reach high"* to connect with those stars?
* What is blocking/stopping you from connecting with those
  - stars
  - passions
  - goals?
* Who might be able to help you locate/get in touch with your hidden Soul-Star(s)?
* How will you know when you have connected with your hidden Soul-Star(s)?

Living Life with Confidence

Soulistry Journal Prompt ... Henry David Thoreau
Go confidently in the direction of your dreams.
Live the life you've imagined.

Soulistry Soul-Questions
* When you were sixteen, what life did you image you'd have when you became an adult?
* Journal about the life you imagine living now if you are not living it.
* What steps can you take to live *"in the direction of your dreams"*
  - emotionally
  - physically
  - intellectually
  - artistically
  - environmentally
  - politically
  - financially
  - spiritually
  - relationally
* How can you not only take steps in the direction of your dreams, but *"go confidently"*?

God's Milk

Soulistry Journal Prompt ... Anne Sexton

There is hope. There is hope everywhere. Today, God gives milk, and I have the pail.

Soulistry Soul-Questions

* Is your soul open to hope - *"hope everywhere"*?
* What do you understand by the phrase *"God gives milk"*?
* How has God/Higher Power/Holy Other/Creator/Spirit given milk in your life?
* How have you responded?
* How can you live your life so that you are ready to receive God's milk of hope in your spiritual pail?
* Are there things in your spiritual pail you need to empty before being able to receive?
* If so, what are they?
* What can you do to prepare your spiritual pail to receive God's *"milk"*?

May You Be Blessed

Soulistry Journal Prompt ... Francis of Assisi

May you be blessed with discomfort at easy answers, half truths and superficial relationships so that you may live deep within your heart. May you be blessed with anger at injustice, oppression and exploitation of people so that you may work for justice, freedom and peace. May you be blessed with tears to shed for those who suffer pain, rejection, hunger and war so that you may reach out your hand to comfort them and turn their pain into joy. And may you be blessed with enough foolishness to believe that you can make a difference in the world so that you can do what others claim cannot be done to bring justice and kindness to all children and the poor.

Soulistry Soul-Questions

* How might you welcome blessings of discomfort *"at easy answers, half truths and superficial relationships so you may live deep within your heart"*?

* How might you welcome blessings of anger *"at injustice, oppression and exploitation of people so that you may work for justice, freedom and peace"*?

* How might you welcome blessings of tears to shed *"for those who suffer pain, rejection, hunger and war so that you may reach out your hand to comfort them and turn their pain into joy"*?

* How might you welcome blessings of foolishness *"to believe that you can make a difference in the world so that you can do what others claim cannot be done to bring justice and kindness to all children and the poor"*?

* Members of Franciscan religious orders follow a lifestyle of simplicity. How might your life be a reflection of that lifestyle? In your Soulistry Journal, reflect on ways you can simplify your life.

What We See

Soulistry Journal Prompt ... Peter Thornton

When you look at your neighbor's work, you see it for what it is.
When you look at your own work, you see it for what it isn't.

Used by permission.

Soulistry Soul-Questions

* Have you ever looked at your own work/art/ project/business/life and seen *"what it isn't"*?
* In your Soulistry Journal, reflect on some moments in your life when you've compared your work, art, projects, efforts in sports activities, hobbies, etc. with another, seen perfection in their work and nothing like it when you've considered your own.
* Do you put pressure on yourself in other areas of your life/relationships? If so, consider an example and write about it in your Soulistry Journal.
* Do others see you as a perfectionist? Are they accurate?
* Does your perfectionism interfere with any of your relationships? If so, how?
* Are you comfortable with this aspect of your personality? If you are not comfortable with being a perfectionist, what might you do to ease up on yourself so that you can spend less time being self-critical?
* When someone expresses appreciation of your work/art/efforts, are you able to reply with sincerity and say "thank you" or is your response apologetic, self-deprecating? In your Soulistry Journal, reflect on why this might be so and what steps you might take to reply with a simply "thank you" the next time someone appreciates your art, your work, your friendship, your gift, you.

Open Doors

Soulistry Journal Prompt ... Alexander Graham Bell

When one door closes, another door opens, but we often look so long and so regretfully upon the closed door, that we do not see the ones which open for us.

Soulistry Soul-Questions

* Reflect on a time in your life when one door seemed to close and another door opened. Did you see the open door?

* Were you caught up in the past and the "what-if's" that might have happened had that door not been closed?

* What about other moments-in-time when one door seemed to close and another opened? Reflect on those in your Soulistry Journal.

* If you were able to open a new door, what learning, blessings, discoveries, challenges, personal growth transpired as a result?

* If Bell's parents had not been hearing-impaired (considered a 'door closed' situation by some), it is unlikely that he would have studied hearing or sound or invented the telephone (door opened). What moments/ incidents/experiences have there been in your life when a closed door resulted in a new direction for your life?

* Reflect on a recent *"closed door"* moment and journal about the blessings that came your way because *"another door"* opened that you hadn't expected.

May 1 Walk

Soulistry Journal Prompt ... Navajo Chants

Happily may I walk. Happily, with abundant dark clouds, may I walk. Happily, with abundant showers, may I walk. Happily, with abundant plants, may I walk. Happily, on a trail of pollen, may I walk. With beauty before me, may I walk. With beauty behind me, may I walk. With beauty above me, may I walk. With beauty below me, may I walk. With beauty all around me, may I walk. Wandering on a trail of beauty, lively I walk.

Soulistry Soul-Questions

* Reflect and journal about moments in your life when you have experienced
  - *"abundant dark clouds"*
  - *"abundant showers"*
  - *"abundant plants"*
  - *"a trail of pollen"*
* How can you *"happily"* walk regardless of outdoor weather conditions or your inner emotional state?
* Consider **your** understanding of walking and the **Navajo** understanding. Is there a difference? If so, what might that be?
* What prevents you from walking Navajo-style on a stroll/in your life?
* What is **your** understanding of *"beauty"*?
* What do you understand the **Navajo** chant understanding of *"beauty"* to be in this Soulistry Journal Prompt?
* When you go for a walk, reflect on the *"beauty"* you see
  - *"before me"*
  - *"behind me"*
  - *"above me"*
  - *"below me"*

Light From Within

Soulistry Journal Prompt ... Elisabeth Kübler-Ross

People are like stained-glass windows. They sparkle and shine when the sun is out, but when the darkness sets in, their true beauty is revealed only if there is a light from within.

Used by permission.

Soulistry Soul-Questions

* What do you understand to be *"the light from within"*?
* What ways might the *"light from within"* be revealed?
* Reflect on a recent time when you 'sparkled and shone'. What was sunny in your life at the time?
* In your Soulistry Journal, reflect on a recent time when *"darkness set in"*. What was dark in your life at that time?
* How did the light that was *"from within"* shine at that dark moment in your life?
* How/when did you recognize that light?
* In your Soulistry Journal, reflect on some of the ways *"true beauty"* has been revealed *"when the darkness"* set in.
* Have you encouraged another in the revelation of their *"true beauty"*? Reflect on that moment in your Soulistry Journal and consider how that experience might be encouragement for your own journey in dark moments.
* What can you do to keep your *"true beauty"* - your *"light from within"* - aflame?
* The Sanskrit greeting 'Namaste' has various meanings, one of which is: *"I honor the light within you."* If you were greeted in such a fashion, how would you interpret that *"light"* that is honored within you by another?
* What *"light"* is within you today?

Courage

Soulistry Journal Prompt ... Ambrose Redmoon

Courage is not the absence of faith, but rather the judgment that something else is more important than fear.

Soulistry Soul-Questions

* How would you define courage?
* Reflect on the last moment in your life when courage was needed. Was it a moment of *"judgment that something else (was) more important than fear"*? If so, what was that *"something else"*?
* Reflect on other moments in your life when courage was needed. How was courage expressed?
* Has courage been expressed the same way each time you've needed it?
* If expressed in different ways, reflect on them in your Soulistry Journal.
* Do you understand emotional courage, physical courage, spiritual courage to be the same, have similar character-istics? In your Soulistry Journal, reflect on what those similarities/ characteristics.
* If that is not your understanding, reflect on what their dissimilarities.
* Is courage something everyone can draw on from within when needed or is courage something only certain people have?
* What do you need courage
  - to face?
  - to do?
  - to believe?
* What prevents you from having the courage that you need?

Finding God's Presence

Soulistry Journal Prompt ... Herbert O'Driscoll

Come and journey, journey upward.
Sing God's praises. Offer prayer.
In the storm and in the stillness
Find God's presence everywhere.

Used by permission.

Soulistry Soul-Questions

* Reflect on moments in your life when you have chosen to *"journey upward"* in your thoughts. Did you *"Sing God's praises"*? *"Offer prayer"*? If so, describe those moments.

* Were you aware of a response to your prayer and praise? If so, what was that response?

* Have you had moments when you experienced *"God's presence everywhere"*? Reflect on those moments in your Soulistry Journal.

* Have your moments of experiencing *"God's presence"* (however you understand God) more often been *"in the storm"* or *"in the stillness"*?

* Is acknowledging *"God's presence"* something you do easily? Describe a recent moment of awareness of God's presence in your Soulistry Journal.

* Describe
  - an *"in the storm"* occasion of awareness of God's presence;
  - an *"in the stillness"* moment;
  - another time when you were aware of the presence of the Holy?

* If you find it difficult to relate to or acknowledge God/Holy Other/Spirit/Creator/Higher Power in your life, difficult to believe in *"God's presence everywhere"*, take

some time to journal about this.

* Has your ability to believe or your difficulty in believing in *"God's presence"* impacted your life in any way i.e. a
  - support group
  - family
  - work
  - friends
  - yourself?
* How have you dealt with this?

Tomorrow's Seeds

Soulistry Journal Prompt ... Chinese Proverb
All the flowers of all the tomorrows are in the seeds of today.

Soulistry Soul-Questions
* How would you explain the *"flowers"* and *"seeds"* metaphor?
* What *"seeds"* are you sowing today for your *"tomorrows"*?
* How are they being sown?
* What *"flowers of all your tomorrows"* are being sown now?

Keeping Secrets

Soulistry Journal Prompt ... Paul Tournier
Nothing makes us so lonely as our secrets.

Used by permission.

Soulistry Soul-Questions
* What secrets lie deep within you?
* Have you ever shared any of those secrets with another? In your Soulistry Journal, reflect on a recent time of secret-sharing.
  - Was your secret kept as a sacred trust?
  - Was your trust betrayed?
* Has someone ever told you a secret and asked you not to tell anyone else? Reflect on your response in your Soulistry Journal.
  - Did you keep that secret?
  - Did you tell that secret to someone else?
* In your Soulistry Journal, reflect on a time when you experienced a time of loneliness. What thoughts/feelings/anxieties did you have?
* How were you able to move beyond that moment/time of loneliness?
* Have you ever experienced loneliness as a result of keeping a secret - your own secret; a family member's secret; a friend's secret? In your Soulistry Journal, reflect on that particular experience of loneliness.
* Are you someone who can keep a secret?

And The Day Came

Soulistry Journal Prompt ... Anaïs Nin

And the day came when the risk to remain tight in the bud was more painful than the risk it took to blossom.

Soulistry Soul-Questions

* Reflect on a moment/situation/decision when you took a risk. Did you remain *"tight in the bud"*? If so, what led to such a state?

* Was remaining *"tight in the bud ... more painful than the risk it took to blossom"*? If so, what blocked your ability to risk?

* In your Soulistry Journal, reflect on times when you were a risk-taker
  - in your relationships
  - at work
  - in your volunteer role
  - in your free-time
  - on your holidays
  - socially
  - financially
  - physically
  - emotionally
  - in life
  - in your art

* Were there consequences to your being a risk-taker? If so, reflect on them in your Soulistry Journal.

* Was there learning in each risk-taking? If so, take a moment to reflect on that in your Soulistry Journal.

* Would you take those same risks again? Reflect on why you would; why you would not.

Rising Every Time

Soulistry Journal Prompt ... Confucius

Our greatest glory is not in never falling, but in rising every time we fall.

Soulistry Soul-Questions

* In your Soulistry Journal, reflect on the moments of *"rising"* in your life. Note what you did to bring about that resurrection moment in your life.
* What were the results?
* Consider a time in your life when stresses were such that you became sad, depressed, isolated, distanced from family/friends/support groups, and did **not** rise. What consequences were there from that time of *"falling"*?
* Have you ever experienced feelings of guilt at times when you were unable to rise after falling? Journal about those feelings and consider how you might handle such feelings should similar occasions arise in the future.
* Reflect on one of the *"rising"* moments in your life in your Soulistry Journal, noting
  - your feelings
  - any consequences
  - what prompted you to rise.
* Reflect on the strength, encouragement, energy, healing you received when you picked yourself up from a difficult time in your life.

Believing

Soulistry Journal Prompt ... Verna Dozier
What difference does it make that you believe?

The Dream of God: A Call to Return; 1991; Cambridge, Massachusetts;

Cowley Publications; page 185. Used by permission.

Soulistry Soul-Questions
* Which is more important for you ... the *"what"* (what you believe) or that believing (in and of itself) makes a difference?
* Why do you think this is so?
* What are your beliefs about
  - the existence of God/Higher Power
  - abortion
  - religion (in general; other religions in particular)
  - capital punishment
  - same-sex blessings/marriage
  - prayer
  - euthanasia

Look Well To This Day

Soulistry Journal Prompt ... Sanskrit Proverb

Yesterday is but a dream and tomorrow is only a vision. But today, well lived, makes every yesterday a dream of happiness and every tomorrow a vision of hope. Look well, therefore, to this day.

Soulistry Soul-Questions

* Would you identify yourself as one who expectantly looks to each day or are you more someone who looks to each day with dread?
* If the latter, what can you do to be more a person who celebrates life?
* Buddhist, Hindu and Jainist proverbs also espouse the philosophy of *"Look well therefore to this day"* and celebrating life. Jewish people often shout *"L'chaim ... to life!"* at special celebrations. Christians and those who are Jewish find encouragement in the Book of Deuteronomy's encouragement to *"Choose life!"* What can you do to make *"every tomorrow a vision of hope"* beginning today?
* In your Soulistry Journal, reflect on how committed you are to taking those little steps. What can you put in place to bring these to reality?
* If you are intentional about changing your attitude about life, are you willing to share this decision with another - a spiritual director, a family member, a soul friend, a counselor, your support group? If not, why not?
* If you are willing to share this decision - with whom and when?

Aging

Soulistry Journal Prompt ... Mark Twain

Age is an issue of mind over matter. If you don't mind, it doesn't matter.

Soulistry Soul-Questions

* When you were ten years of age, how old was 'old'? When you were twenty – forty – sixty, how old was 'old'?

* Reflect on the aging process, and journal about your concerns, hopes, fears, expectations for the future.

* If you didn't know your real age, how old do you think you would be today: physically, intellectually, spiritually, chronologically?

* If those ages reflect an age older than you really are, what might you do to lower that age and bring it closer to your real age?

* If age really is *"an issue of mind over matter"*, do you mind being the age you now are? If so, what concerns do you have
  - physically
  - intellectually
  - financially
  - spiritually
  - relationally

Aiming High

Soulistry Journal Prompt ...... Michelangelo

The greatest danger for most of us is not that our aim is too high and we miss it, but that it is too low and we reach it.

Soulistry Soul-Questions

* What aims/goals have you had in the past?
* Did you achieve them all? Reflect on this in your Soulistry Journal.
* What *"aims"* (goals) have you set for yourself for the coming year?
  - the next three years
  - the next five years
  - the next ten years
* Reflect on each goal (*"aim"*) and time frame in your Soulistry Journal. Would you describe each as realistic? manageable? unrealistic? unmanageable? How so?
* When you aimed *"too low"*, what factors contributed in the setting of those goals?
* What blocks you from setting achievable, higher goals?
* Have you set any *"aims"*/goals that were *"too low"*? If so, what can you do to aim higher when setting future *"aims"*/goals?
* Reflect on your *"aims"* (goals) for the next twelve months. What can you do to bring them to fruition?

Draw The Circle Wide

Soulistry Journal Prompt ... Gordon Light

Draw the circle wide. Draw it wider still.
Let this be our song, no one stands alone, standing side by side.
Draw the circle wide.

Used by permission.

Soulistry Soul-Questions

* Reflect on moments in your life when you stood alone. Select one of these moments and journal about the
  - situation
  - your thoughts
  - your feelings at the time.

* Was there someone (individual, support group, family member, friend, acquaintance, spiritual director, counselor, clergy person, physician, AA sponsor, police officer, etc.) you could have turned to; someone you could have shared your anxiety, your joy, your pain, your fear – but didn't? In your Soulistry Journal, reflect on who that person (persons) might have been and consider why you did not reach out.

* Reflect on a moment in your life when you widened your circle so that another/others could stand *"side by side"* with you. Make some time to journal your feelings about that experience.

* How can your circle widen?

Loving Your Enemy

Soulistry Journal Prompt ... Jesus of Nazareth
Love your enemies and pray for those who persecute you. If you love only those who love you, what good is that? If you are kind only to your friends, how are you different from anyone else?

Matthew chapter 5, verses 44a, 46-47

Soulistry Soul-Questions
* Who have been/are people you would classify as your enemy?
* Why do you think of them in this way?
* What might a prayer for *"those who persecute you"* look like?
* In your Soulistry Journal, reflect on the meaning of *"love"* when it comes to loving your enemies.
* Think of an enemy you have been **able** to love. In your Soulistry Journal, reflect on what transpired to bring you to this point of understanding?
* Think of an enemy you are **unable** to love. Reflect on how you might be able to move to a posture of love for this person.

Soul-Harvest

Soulistry Journal Prompt ... Lao Tzu

Nurturing your love is like tending a small garden. If you keep pulling up the plants to see if the roots are growing, you will not harvest anything.

Soulistry Soul-Questions

* Are you someone who is more likely to *"nurture"* or *"pull up"* - be that your art, relationships, yourself?
* Reflect on times in your life when you have engaged in self-nurture. How did you do that?
* What results/consequences were there?
* Spend some time reflecting on times in your life when you continually *"pulled up the plants to see if anything was growing"*. Were these times of self-examination so that you could learn from your experiences? Were they times of self-recrimination and reproach?
* What results/consequences were there?
* In your Soulistry Journal, reflect on a recent nurturing-harvest-time in your life when you discovered rich soul-harvest as a result.
* Reflect on the times in your life when you nurtured your love like *"tending a small garden"*. What did you do? What resulted?

Vulnerability

Soulistry Journal Prompt ... Sigmund Freud
Out of your vulnerabilities will come your strength.

Soulistry Soul-Questions
* In your Soulistry Journal, reflect on your vulnerabilities. What are they?
* Over the years, have they increased? diminished? disappeared? remained the same?
* Reflect how they have increased/diminished/disappeared /remained the same.
* Have your vulnerabilities affected your ability to deal with life's moments of emotional fragility? Reflect on this in your Soulistry Journal.
* Have you ever experienced your vulnerabilities to be crippling? Journal about one of those moments and what prevented them from becoming strengths in that situation.
* Consider a moment when strength has come *"out of your vulnerabilities"* and journal about your thoughts, feelings and the results of that moment.
* What can you do in the future so that your vulnerabilities are more *"strength"* and less disability?

A Spirituality Of Work

Soulistry Journal Prompt ... Confucius
If you enjoy what you do, you'll never work another day in your life.

Soulistry Soul-Questions
* What does *"work"* mean for you?
* Reflect on your work experiences over the years. Did you enjoy what you did?
* How would you describe/explain a spirituality of work?
* If you receive an income for work that you do, is the work enjoyable or is it a means to an end? If your work is not enjoyable, what can you do to change that?
* Is what you do to earn an income, congruent with something about which you feel passionately?
* What is it about *"what you do"* that you *"enjoy"*?
* What steps can you take to bring enjoyment/passion into what you do if it is not already there in some way?

Today's Road

Soulistry Journal Prompt ... traditionally attributed to Nagarjuna

I always knew that one day I would take this road, but yesterday I did not know that today would be the day.

Soulistry Soul-Questions

* When you were younger *("yesterday")*, what roads did you think you would take?
  - vocationally
  - socially
  - professionally
  - financially
  - relationally
* Have you taken any of those roads yet?
* What *"today"* became *"the day"* for you?
* In each of these areas, was the road-you-took as you imagined it would be? How so?
* If roads have not been taken, what do you need to do for that to happen?
* How do the tomorrows, the todays, and the yesterdays of your life flow?
* Is there congruence, connection, gentleness or is there anxiety? If there is anxiety, what might you do so that the anxiety is lessened?
* What is the road you are on at this moment in your life?

Friend Near And Far Away

Soulistry Journal Prompt ... Kahlil Gibran

A friend who is far away is sometimes much nearer than one who is at hand. Is not the mountain far more awe-inspiring and more clearly visible to one passing through the valley than to those who inhabit the mountain?

Soulistry Soul-Questions

* As you consider people you have considered friends over the years, what common qualities/characteristics do they share?

* How do you distinguish a friend from an acquaintance?

* Have you ever been betrayed by a friend? In your Soulistry Journal, reflect about the circumstances and consequences of that friend's betrayal.

* In your world of friends over the years, what distinguishes those you would call 'close' friend and those you would call 'best' friend?

* Social media (i.e. Facebook, LinkedIn, Twitter) connects people as 'friends'. Is social media another category of friendship for you and if so, what qualities/characteristics do such friends have which distinguish them from other friends?

* Picture your best friend. What is it about this person that draws you to him/her?

* In your circle of friendships over the years, have some friends changed categories — i.e. acquaintance, close friend, best friend, acquaintance, cyber-friend? If so, reflect your role in the changing friendship.

* Reflect on a relationship you have with a *"friend who is far away"*. Is that person *"nearer than the one who is at hand"* and if so, how?

Holding Fast to Dreams

Soulistry Journal Prompt ... Langston Hughes
Hold fast to dreams, for if dreams die, life is a broken winged bird that cannot fly.

Soulistry Soul-Questions
* What dreams have you had for your life?
* Have they all come to fruition?
* Have you had to let go of any of those dreams?
* In reflecting on that letting-go-time, has there been 'death' or 'life' because of the cessation of your dream? Reflect on your response in your Soulistry Journal.
* What dreams do you have for the rest of your life?
* What dreams have you been able to *"hold fast"*?

Feeding the Wolf

Soulistry Journal Prompt ... Cherokee legend

A Cherokee elder sitting with his grandchildren told them this story. "In everyone's life, there is a terrible daily fight—a fight between two wolves. One wolf is evil. This one is negativity, fear, anger, envy, greed, arrogance, self-pity, resentment, frustration, boredom and deceit. The other wolf is good. This one is joy, serenity, self-control, humility, goodness, confidence, generosity, truth, kindness, gentleness, love, patience and compassion." A child asked, "Grandfather, which wolf wins the fight?" The elder looked him in the eye. "The one you feed."

Soulistry Soul-Questions

* Which wolf do you feed in your life most often - the *"good"* wolf or the *"evil"* wolf?
* How have you fed that wolf?
* If you are feeding the evil wolf, are you content nourishing this aspect within your soul?
* If not, how can you feed the wolf that nurtures your spirit; encourages you to be hope-filled, joyful and peace-filled; and motivates you to be more pro-active with your spiritual growth?
* How have you fed the *"good"* wolf? In your Soulistry Journal, reflect on a situation when the good wolf defeated the evil wolf.

Spiritual Mountain-Climbing

Soulistry Journal Prompt ... Sri Chinmoy
Spirituality is constant inner mountain-climbing.

Soulistry Soul-Questions
* How would you define spirituality?
* What do you understand *"constant inner mountain-climbing"* to mean?
* What *"inner mountain-climbing"* have you experienced? In your Soulistry Journal, reflect on a recent experience and the results of *"inner mountain-climbing"*.
* How can *"constant"* inner mountain-climbing be expressed in your life?
* Are there other elements to your understanding of spirituality? If so, reflect on them in your Soulistry Journal.

Doing What You Think You Cannot Do

Soulistry Journal Prompt ... Eleanor Roosevelt

You gain strength, courage and confidence by every experience in which you really stop to look fear in the face. You must do the thing which you think you cannot do.

Used by permission.

Soulistry Soul-Questions

* Reflect on a moment in your life when you gained *"strength, courage and confidence"* by looking *"fear in the face."* Describe the situation in your Soulistry Journal and what steps you took to overcome the fear you felt.

* Were others involved in helping you in that situation? In your Soulistry Journal, reflect on who they were and what role they played.

* It's often said that 'naming your fears' is half the battle in overcoming fears. Reflect on fears you have had in your life (as a child, adolescent, young adult, newly-wed, parent, widow/widower, senior) and name/write them in your Soulistry Journal. Give yourself time and space as you process those fears. Perhaps this 'first step' in facing your fears will give you courage to move to the next step.

* If you can move to the next step in facing your fears, what might that involve?

* If you are unable to name your fears or unable to move to the next step in facing your fears, reflect on this blockage and consider talking about it with a trusted friend, counselor, AA sponsor, spiritual director/soul friend.

* Are there any things in your life now *"which you think you cannot do"*?

* What might those be?

* How might you *"do the thing which you think you cannot do"*,

* How might you get to a point of *"celebrating the strength, courage and confidence"* you gain by looking *"fear in the face"*.

The Only Journey

Soulistry Journal Prompt ... Rainer Maria Rilke
The only journey is the one within.

Soulistry Soul-Questions

* If the *"only journey is the one within"* how can one go *"within"* oneself?
* What do you hope to discover as you go within?
* Reflect on times when you have journeyed within yourself. What have you discovered?
* Have those times resulted in growth, learning, change, stagnation? In your Soulistry Journal, reflect on those times and the results.
* Reflect on times when you have chosen **not** to journey within yourself. What brought you to such a decision? What resulted?
* Do you agree with Rilke's statement that the *"only"* journey is inward? Reflect on times when you have journeyed with the help of another ... family member, friend, spouse, prayer group, spiritual director, counselor, AA sponsor, support group, Quaker friends, your partner, others.
* How might Rilke's words address
  - societal spiritual issues
  - personal spiritual issues
  - environmental issues
* Reflect on the differences between journeying within by yourself and journeying with the help of another.

Hatred Ceases

Soulistry Journal Prompt ... Siddhārtha Gautama (Buddha)

Hatred does not cease through hatred at any time. Hatred ceases through love.

Soulistry Soul-Questions

* Reflect on times when you have felt hatred welling-up within you. In your Soulistry Journal, describe the situation:
  - who was involved;
  - what was underneath the hatred;
  - how it felt;
  - what were the circumstances
* Would you consider your hatred to be sufficiently strong that others would identify you as a sexist, racist, ageist, etc?
* If so, is this a position with which you are comfortable? In your Soulistry Journal, reflect on how you feel about having such a label put on you.
* Have you able to move beyond your hatred? How did you do that?
* If you have been unable to move beyond your hatred, can you get to the reason why that happened? Spend time reflecting about this and consider talking about it with a counselor, support group, spiritual director/soul friend.
* Reflect on times when you have felt another's hatred of what you stood for; for what you believed; for what you did; how you expressed/represented yourself; the color of your skin; the language you spoke; the religion you followed; the political position or politician you supported; your height; your weight; your gender; something else.

In each of these situations
- Who was involved?
- What was underneath the hatred?
- How did it feel?
- What were the circumstances?

* Would you consider that person's hatred of you to be sufficiently strong that you would identify him/her as a sexist, racist, ageist etc?

* How did you deal with being the object of another's hatred?

* If anger, hatred, fear of this person is still with you, how might you move on with your life so that the hatred ceases?

* Reflect on how *"hatred ceases through love"* in your life.

Walking In and Out

Soulistry Journal Prompt ... Joy Harjo

I walk in and out of many worlds.

Soulistry Soul-Questions

* What *"world(s)"* do you *"walk in and out of"* most days?
* Might Harjo's *"worlds"* be interchangeable with the 'houses, mansions, rooms, dwellings' used by translators of John 14: 2 - 6 in the Christian Bible? How so?
* Might these words speak about a life-after-life that the Creator offers? Might they speak about a life here on earth that we create - e.g. the house (world) of negativity: of anger, despair, self-pity, indifference, resignation, frustration, unforgiveness – or the house (world) of positivity: of hope, enthusiasm, cooperation, love, giving, compassion, love, joy, helping others etc.? Reflect on these possibilities in your Soulistry Journal.
* Reflect on how ultimate destiny in the world/house is predicated by action/thoughts here on earth?
* Reflect on why you/others choose to live in certain houses/worlds and not in others each day or during moments of certain days: houses of negativity rather than hope; houses of anger rather than love, etc?
* What rooms/houses/worlds would you like to inhabit that you ordinarily don't inhabit?
* What can you do to change your walk *"in and out of"* worlds (rooms/homes) that will nourish and nurture your spirit, enrich your relationship?
* What world/house will you choose to live in this day?

Radiating Intrinsic Goodness

Soulistry Journal Prompt ... Wangari Maathai

We can work together for a better world with men and women of goodwill, those who radiate the intrinsic goodness of humankind.

Used by permission.

Soulistry Soul-Questions

* What does *"intrinsic goodness of humankind"* mean to you?
* How can *"intrinsic goodness"* be radiated?
* How can spirituality be expressed in environmental, economic, political etc. activism?
* How can you work together with others who *"radiate the intrinsic goodness of humankind"* for *"a better world"*?

The Art of Being Kind

Soulistry Journal Prompt ... Ella Wheeler Wilcox

So many gods, so many creeds, so many paths that wind and wind while just the art of being kind is all the sad world needs.

Soulistry Soul-Questions

* How would you define the *"art of being kind"*?
* What does religion (*"so many gods, so many creeds, so many paths that wind and wind"*) bring to the world?
* What has religion brought to you?
* Reflect and journal about specific ways you can express kindness
  - with family members – immediate and extended
  - with work colleagues
  - in your community
  - with strangers
  - in the world

Hope Has Two Daughters

Soulistry Journal Prompt ... Augustine

Hope has two daughters. Their names are anger and courage; anger at the way things are and courage to see that they do not remain the way they are.

Soulistry Soul-Questions

* Reflect on a moment in your life when you needed hope, and hope came. In your Soulistry Journal, describe
  - the situation
  - your thoughts
  - your feelings when hope became real
  - how that hope manifested itself in you
* Remembering a moment in your life when you needed hope, and hope was distant, journal about
  - the situation
  - your thoughts
  - your feelings during the situation
* Were anger and courage manifested in you? How?
* When life ebbs and flows and there are difficult moments when hopelessness seems present, what/who gives you hope?
  - in personal situations and relationships?
  - in global situations?

Success

Soulistry Journal Prompt ... Henry Ward Beecher
One's best success comes after their greatest disappointments.

Soulistry Soul-Questions
* How would you define *"success"*?
* Reflect and journal about moments in your life when success has come after disappointment.
  - What were the disappointments?
  - What were the successes?
* Do the following enter into an understanding of *"success"* for you? If so, in your Soulistry Journal, reflect on each of them as a qualification for success.
  - financial reward
  - educational degree
  - title
  - workplace promotion
  - material possessions
  - workplace raises/bonuses

Worldly Inexperience

Soulistry Journal Prompt ... Joseph Addison

Prejudice and self-sufficiency naturally proceed from inexperience of the world and ignorance.

Soulistry Soul-Questions

* How does Addison's explanation of the evolution of prejudice and self-sufficiency compare with your under-standing?

* Can you think of incidents in your life when your worldly inexperience and ignorance affected you so that another (others) said you were prejudiced? Reflect on one of those incidents in your Soulistry Journal and how it felt to have the label of 'prejudice' applied to you.
  - Did you agree with their comment? Were you able to acknowledge your prejudice?

* In your mind, is prejudice the umbrella word for "ism's" (racism, able-ism, ageism, etc.) or is it something completely different? Reflect on that in your Soulistry Journal.

* Do you believe the educational system has a role in moving people from ignorance (of the world) to knowledge (of political systems, historical realities, health concerns, environmental/religious/racial/economic issues?) If so, what would be that role?

Rekindling the Light

Soulistry Journal Prompt ... Albert Schweitzer

Sometimes our light goes out, but is blown into flame by another human being. Each of us owes deepest thanks to those who have rekindled this light.

Used by permission.

Soulistry Soul-Questions

* In your Soulistry Journal, reflect on one of the times when your *"light"* went out. What were the circumstances?
* How did your light ignite again? Was it *"blown into flame by another human being"*? If so, how?
* Have you expressed appreciation to that person for their action/words?
* If so, how did you do that?
* If not, reflect and journal about some ways you might do so – perhaps beginning today.

Seeing the Spirit Sparkle

Soulistry Journal Prompt ... Gwen Weaver

Are any of us perfect? I don't think so. I would rather like to see the spirit. It's the sparkle in the eye - the slight opening of the soul.

Used by permission.

Soulistry Soul-Questions

* Describe a recent moment in your life when you set perfection as your goal rather than allowing the spirit to flow through you.

* How might you allow your next project/assignment/ performance/presentation to be less intentional about 'skill and understanding' and more intentional about enjoying the moment/the performance/ the work/the presentation/ the assignment?

* How might you be more open to discovering and uncovering the *"sparkle in the eye"* of the soul of your
  - artistic endeavors
  - daily chores
  - relationships
  - spirituality

* How can you *"see the spirit"* in another?

What Does Love Look Like

Soulistry Journal Prompt ... Augustine

What does love look like? It has the hands to help others. It has the feet to hasten to the poor and needy. It has eyes to see misery and want. It has the ears to hear the sighs and sorrow. That is what love looks like.

Soulistry Soul-Questions

* The ancient Greeks had four words for love: *agápē* (unconditional love); *érōs* (intimate love); *philía* (friendship love); and *storgē* (natural affection such as felt by parents for children). In your Soulistry Journal, reflect on how you have expressed love in the past for family, friend, colleague, stranger, the world.

* Was the love you showed expressed verbally, monetarily, physically, emotionally, politically, prayerfully, in an action-oriented way, simply by your presence, a visit, a card, a phone call, an email?

* Journal about an incident where the love you felt was expressed with the
  - *"hands to help"*
  - *"feet to hasten to the poor and needy"*
  - *"eyes to see misery and want"*
  - *"ears to hear the sighs and sorrow"*

* Are words sufficient to express love or are actions also an integral part of expressing love? In your Soulistry Journal, consider a situation with someone you say you love, but the other receives a different message because your actions don't reflect the words.

* What can you do to bring the love you say you have for an individual so that they feel loved by you in both word and action?

* Consider ways you might express your love that are different from the ways you have expressed love in the

past.

* In your Soulistry Journal, reflect on situations when you have felt loved – deeply loved – by a parent, child, partner, spouse, God, pet, stranger. What did *"love look like"*?

Deepening the Mystery

Soulistry Journal Prompt ... Francis Bacon

The job of the artist is always to deepen the mystery.

Used by permission.

Soulistry Soul-Questions

* What does *"the mystery"* mean to you?
* What gift of creativity have you been given?
* What defines/makes someone an *"artist"*?
* When you express yourself in some creative way, do you think of yourself as an *"artist"*? If not, what would it take for you to see yourself as an artist (someone who bakes, sews, sculpts, paints, does carpentry/flower-arranging, makes cards, gardens, calligraphically-renders words, draws, sews, etc.).
* How can you, as artist, *"deepen the mystery"*?

Keening

Soulistry Journal Prompt ... Lars

Suffering lost in itself, the song lost in the song: keening sounds over the plain.

Used by permission.

An aside: Keening (from the Irish 'caoine' meaning 'to lament') is understood as lamenting/mourning in a loud wailing voice.

Soulistry Soul-Questions

* When/what was the occasion you experienced such suffering that it was *"lost in itself"*?
* Have you ever expressed grief/pain/sadness/loneliness/shame/alienation/guilt/loss such that it would *"sound over the plain"*?
* If so, was a connection with a deeper part of yourself (perhaps with Holy Other /God /By Whatever Name) that brought you some sense of healing in that time of keening?
* What do you understand to be the *"song"*?
* What does *"lost in the song"* mean to you?
* When your song has been *"lost in the song"*, what has prevented you from keening?
* How have you responded to suffering in your lifetime?
* How have you grieved? In your Soulistry Journal, reflect on grieving times i.e. loss of employment, relationship, limb, loved one, health, pet.
* Were you able to move beyond grieving the loss and if so, how did that come about?
* If you've not been able to move beyond grieving a particular loss, consider ways you might begin to do so.

Forgiveness

Soulistry Journal Prompt ... Mahatma Gandhi

If we practice an eye for an eye and a tooth for a tooth, soon the whole world will be blind and toothless.

Soulistry Soul-Questions

* Reflect on a moment in your life when another hurt you. Was forgiveness something that came easily to you or were you wanting to "get even"?

* Has there been a moment when you wanted to practice *"an eye for an eye and a tooth for a tooth"*? In your Soulistry Journal, reflect on such a moment – describe the situation, your response, how you felt.

* If you were able to move beyond the hurt and pain another caused you to forgiveness of that person, what helped you to do so?

* Does forgiving the person mean forgetting the incident? If not, then in the remembering, is the pain still there? And if the pain is still there, is there something you can do to move beyond the physical/emotional/spiritual bondage between you and the other? What might that be?

* Think of a time when you caused another to be hurt, upset and s/he responded with forgiveness. What learning has come from that time?

* How is the relationship between you and that other person? Has it continued, flourished, ended?

* Have you ever experienced a situation when another was hurt by your actions, thoughts, words? In time, they forgave you, but you did not forgive yourself. Spend some time with your Soulistry Journal considering what you can do to forgive yourself.

Laughing At Ourselves

Soulistry Journal Prompt ... Katherine Mansfield

When we can begin to take our failures seriously, it means we are ceasing to be afraid of them. It is of immense importance to learn to laugh at ourselves.

Soulistry Soul-Questions

* How would you define 'failure' in general? How would you define it for your life?
* Reflect on some failures in your life. Were they points of blockage or points of learning?
* Consider one failure that blocked your growth and inhibited your willingness to risk trying again. Spend some time journaling about this situation.
* Consider one failure which you took seriously and ceased *"to be afraid"* of its hold over you. How did you get to that point?
* What consequences emerged?
* Does laughing at yourself come naturally to you or is it something you must work at or learn?
* Reflect on a recent time in your life when you laughed at yourself. What was the situation? What did you learn about yourself?

Problem-Solving

Soulistry Journal Prompt ... Anthony D'Angelo
When solving problems, dig at the roots instead of just hacking at the leaves.

Soulistry Soul-Questions
* How do you solve problems that come up in your life?
* In your Soulistry Journal, reflect on the two problem-solving methods: root-digger and leaf-hacker. How would you describe them?
* What are the advantages of each?
* What are the disadvantages of each?
* Describe incidents when you have solved a problem the **leaf-hacking** way and reflect on the consequences of your action.
* Describe incidents when you have solved problems the **root-digging** way and reflect on the consequences of your action.
* Does problem-solving have an impact on your spiritual life?* How?

Trusting the Unseen

Soulistry Journal Prompt ... Ralph Waldo Emerson

All I have seen teaches me to trust the Creator for all I have not seen.

Soulistry Soul-Questions

* Is 'trusting the unseen' a gift or is it something one can cultivate?

* Are you a trusting person? If so, how is trust expressed in your daily life?

* What steps could one take to become able *"to trust the Creator"*?

* In your Soulistry Journal, reflect on the different levels of trust:
  - trust of friends
  - trust of strangers
  - trust of the government
  - trust of family
  - trust of self

* What have you *"seen"* that invites you to trust the existence of God/Holy Other/Higher Power/Spirit/ Creator?

* What have you seen that moves you beyond considering the 'possibility of existence' to an 'abiding awareness' of a Higher Power?

* What are the have-not-seen's for which you have no certainty?

* Which of the have-not-seen's, because of being able to trust the Creator for all of the things-seen, are you are able to believe?

The Idea of God

Soulistry Journal Prompt ... traditionally attributed to
Madeleine L'Engle though original authorship is likely that of
Miguel de Unamuno

*Those who believe that they believe in God, but without passion in
their hearts, without anguish of mind, without uncertainty, without
doubt, without an element of despair even in their consolation, believe
only in the God-Idea, not God.*

Soulistry Soul-Questions

* Have there been moments in your life when your belief in
  a Higher Power was based on *"passion in the heart"*? Take
  a moment to reflect and journal about those times. What
  resulted in your growth as a spiritual being?
* It's been said that there are no atheists in foxholes in war.
  Have there been moments in your life when you drew
  close(er) to belief in a Higher Power?
* If so, were those moments when you were experiencing
  "anguish of mind ... even at times despair"? Reflect on those
  moments in your Soulistry Journal.
* What about moments of *"uncertainty"* and *"doubt"*? Take a
  moment to reflect and journal about some of those
  moments. What did they produce in terms of your spiritu-
  ality?
* Have there been moments when you believed only in the
  "idea *of God"* and *"not **in** God"*?
* Did those moments sustain you in times of crisis, stress,
  difficulty?
* How did they?
* What is it you believe about God/Higher Power/
  Creator/G_d/Holy Other/Spirit?

A Spiritual Experience

Soulistry Journal Prompt ... Pierre Teillard de Chardin

We are not human beings having a spiritual experience. We are spiritual beings having a human experience.

Soulistry Soul-Questions

* What is your understanding of *"spiritual beings"*?
* What is your understanding of *"spiritual experiences"*?
* How does de Chardin's position (*"spiritual beings having a human experience"*) differ from the *"human beings having a spiritual experience"* perspective?
* To which position do you ascribe? What brings you to such a conclusion?
* What difference would it make for you to live each day from one position or the other?

Darkness Deserves Gratitude

Soulistry Journal Prompt ... Joan Chittister

Darkness deserves gratitude. It is the alleluia point at which we learn to understand that all growth does not take place in the sunlight.

"Uncommon Gratitude: Alleluia for All That Is"

(co-authored with Rowan Williams) Used by permission.

Soulistry Soul-Questions

* Reflect on some moments of darkness in your life. While you were experiencing those moments, was gratitude for the darkness something you expressed at the time? If so, describe what you were grateful for.

* Are there moments of darkness in your life when you did not express gratitude at the time, but looking back at that moment you can relate to it as being an *"alleluia point"* when you learned to understand that *"all growth does not take place in the sunlight"?* Take time to journal your expressions of gratitude now.

* Were those moments a time of growth? In your Soulistry Journal, reflect on what kind of growth emerged.

* What have you learned from moments of darkness that encourage you to move out of the darkness into the light with deeper self-knowledge, self-awareness and self-confidence?

Blessed Are You

Soulistry Journal Prompt ... Jesus of Nazareth

Blessed are the peacemakers for they shall be called the children of God.

Matthew chapter 5, verse 9

Soulistry Soul-Questions

* In your Soulistry Journal, reflect on the 'who, what, when, why, where' of incidents in your life when you have been the recipient of a peacemaker's activity in:
  - your family
  - society
  - war time
  - a confrontational workplace setting
* What characteristics best describe those who are peacemakers in your family, among your friends, in society, during wartime, in relationships, in the world?
* Reflect on a situation when you have functioned as a peacemaker. How did you become involved?
* What was the outcome?
* How did you feel during the process?
* Jesus uses the word *"blessed"* in relationship with peacemakers. As you reflect on this word, what images and thoughts emerge for you?
* What does being called a child of God (*"children of God"*) mean to you?

Gladdening The Hearts

Soulistry Journal Prompt ... Henri Amiel

Life is short and we do not have much time to gladden the hearts of those who travel the way with us. So, be swift to love and make haste to be kind.

Soulistry Soul-Questions

* Amiel refers to *"those who travel the way with us"*. To what do you think he was referring?
* Have you been conscious of *"gladdening the hearts"* of others in your life?
* In your Soulistry Journal, reflect on such an instance/occasion. Was this act conscious or unconscious?
* How would you define *"love"* in Amiel's context?
* How can you be (more) *"swift to love"* in your life?
* How can you *"make haste to be kind"* with:
  - your colleagues at work
  - family members
  - friends
  - acquaintances
  - strangers
  - enemies
  - yourself

Six Letters

Soulistry Journal Prompt ... Gemma Black
Silent - Listen: Six letters. Two words. One meaning.

Used by permission

Soulistry Soul-Questions
* Do you find it easy to be silent?
* Is silence something you welcome or something you resent?
* What role has silence played in your life: in your spiritual journey; in your daily life; in your artistic and creative expression?
* If silence has not played a part in your spiritual/ daily/artistic/creative life, what might be blocking your ability to do so?
* How might you cultivate silence (more silence) in your life?
* Have you ever been involved in clowning as a 'silent clown'? In your Soulistry Journal, reflect on how such a use of silence might contribute to your spiritual growth.
* Is there a difference between 'listening' and 'hearing' and if so, what is that difference?
* Do others perceive you to be a good listener? Do you see yourself that way when it comes to listening to others, listening to that 'still, small voice within', listening to God/Higher Power/Spirit?
* Reflect on your understanding of what the two words:*"one meaning"* conveys.
* Take a moment now to be silent and listen. What do you hear? Draw, paint, calligraph, sculpt, design, create something expressing the essence of this time of silent listening. Blog/write in your Soulistry Journal about what you are hearing as you listen and are silent.

All Shall Be Well

Soulistry Journal Prompt ... Julian of Norwich

All shall be well. All shall be well. And all manner of things shall be well.

Soulistry Soul-Questions

* What do you think Dame Julian was referring to in her use of the word *"all"*?
* Can *"all"* be well in one's personal world? If so, what would it take for that to be a reality?
* Can *"all"* be well in the world? If so, what would it take for that to be a reality?
* Consider a crisis time in your life when belief in Dame Julian's words would have brought you comfort. Describe and reflect on that time in your Soulistry Journal.
* How might Dame Julian's words equip you to deal with awkward moments, difficult people, impossible situations?

A Meditation

* *Take a moment and close your eyes. Get into a comfortable position. Focus on your breathing — let it become deep, slow, gentle.*
* *Think of a situation (personal/global) or an individual where anxiety, fear, stress became real for you.*
* *Envision yourself with that person/situation, where you are protected and safe.*
* *Remember to breathe deeply and focus on feeling safe and protected.*
* *In your mind or out loud, repeat Dame Julian's words several times, remembering to breathe gently and deeply.*

* *As you inhale, breathe in all that is good, holy, peaceful, healing. As you exhale, breathe out negative thoughts, unpleasant feelings, bad memories.*

* *As you begin to open your eyes, gently stretch your arms, neck, shoulders, legs, feet as you breathe in goodness, wholeness and peace.*

In your Soulistry Journal, reflect on your experience of the brief meditation and record how repeating Dame Julian's words might bring a sense of calm to you in future difficult moments or encounters.

The Acquisition of Wisdom

Soulistry Journal Prompt ... Solomon ibn Gabirol
The first step in the acquisition of wisdom is silence, the second listening, the third memory, the fourth practice, the fifth teaching others.

Soulistry Soul-Questions

* Gabirol cites *"silence ... listening ... memory ... practice ... and teaching others"* as components of wisdom. How do you think these affect the acquisition of wisdom?
* If there other components you would add, what would they be?
* Are there components as defined by Gabirol you would remove from a listing of steps-to-acquire-wisdom? Which ones might they be and why would you include them?
* Reflect on the lives of some people you consider to be wise. What is it about their lives, actions, beliefs that would motivate you to describe them in such a way?
* Reflect on moments in your own life when you have been aware of wisdom coming from you.
* Reflect on moments when others have named wisdom as one of your attributes. In your Soulistry Journal, describe the situation, your response, what you were feeling at those moments.

Gratitude

Soulistry Journal Prompt ... Meister Eckhart
If the only prayer you say is thank you, that would suffice.

Soulistry Soul-Questions
* Are you able to say *"thank-you"* to the Creator/God/Holy Other/Spirit for at least one thing in your life that encourages you each day?
* What is the first thing that comes to mind when you offer this prayer/say this affirmation?
* As you reflect on having an attitude of gratitude, what other things come to mind?
* What about people - who are you grateful for and why are you grateful for them?
* How can you express your gratitude to these people?
* In your Soulistry Journal, reflect on some of the blessings in your life and note how you express gratitude for:
  - gift of intellect
  - ability to see, hear, taste, touch, swallow, breathe
  - ability to blink your eyes, move your limbs, speak, feel emotions
  - shelter; food; medical care
  - eyeglasses; hearing aids
  - availability of medication; walker; scooter
  - family: immediate family; extended family; deceased family members
  - friends: close friends; friends at work; friends in other places
  - gainful employment; transportation
  - volunteer opportunities
  - money in the bank; money in your pocket
  - water to drink; food to eat; good air to breathe

*   Reflect on which of the above you take for granted.

A Gratitude/Blessing Jar

Before going to bed each night, note one thing/incident/person for which you feel grateful (with or without a comment) on a slip of paper and place it in a special jar/box.

On your next birthday, remove the slips of paper from the jar and look at them - "seeing" your life from the perspective of blessing ... things for which you have been grateful.

Note the 'surprising' blessings of the past year in your Soulistry Journal – record the date.

As the years pass, refer back to your list of blessings from previous years and note similarities, new blessings. An attitude of gratitude is a gentle way to nurture your spirituality.

Religious Belief

Soulistry Journal Prompt ... Dalai Lama

My religion is very simple. My religion is kindness. Practice kindness whenever it is possible. It is always possible.

Used by permission.

Soulistry Soul-Questions

* When you think of religion, what images come to mind?
* Reflect on your involvement with religious institutions over the years ... the joyful, meaningful and soul-giving moments that nurtured your spirituality ... the moments of frustration, anger, guilt. Do those moments nurture your spirit or block your spiritual growth? How so?
* Where are you now in terms of involvement with a religious institution? Are you active – on the fringe – uninvolved?
* If you are uninvolved or only marginally involved, what do you think of the Dalai Lama's understanding of religion?
* When you do a random act of kindness, is it as an extension of your spirituality – your religion? Something else? Reflect on this in your Soulistry Journal.
* Has practicing kindness been *"always possible"* in your life and if so, have you done so?
* If there have been moments when you have not practiced the religion of kindness, consider:
  - who was involved
  - what prevented you from being kind
  - what you could do to make amends to this person

Soul-Alive

Soulistry Journal Prompt .... Eleonora Duse

If the sight of blue skies fills you with joy; if a blade of grass springing up in the fields has power to move you; if the simple things of nature have a message that you understand, rejoice, for your soul is alive!

Soulistry Soul-Questions

* What does the word *"joy"* convey to you?
* What *"fills you with joy"* at this point in your life?
* What has filled you with joy at other times in your life?
* What/who has power *"to move you"*?
* If you were to describe your soul as *"alive"*, reflect in your Soulistry Journal on what contributed to that state and how it felt.
* If you were to describe your soul in another way (stagnant/blocked/other), journal what that felt like.
* What would it take to have your soul to come alive?
* When was the most recent time when *"simple things of nature"* had a message that you understood?
* Reflect on a time when you were able to enjoy *"the simple things of nature"*- a walk in a park, quiet time looking at cloud formations, a rainbow, smelling a rose etc. Consider how these experiences might have encouraged an alive soul within you ... even if only for a moment.
* In your Soulistry Journal, reflect on moments when *"the simple things of nature"* had *"a message"* that you understood.

Today I Am Asking

Soulistry Journal Prompt .... Alice Hancock

*Today I am asking you to help one, to cheer one, to give hope to one —
yourself.*

Used by permission.

Soulistry Soul-Questions

* When you first read the above words, did you expect the ending to be the single word: *"yourself"*? How did you anticipate it would end?
* Reflect on moments in your life when you extended yourself to others while overlooking/disregarding your own needs.
* How can you balance self-care with being present to others?
* How can you *"help ... cheer ... give hope"* to yourself today?
* How can you be more intentional about self-care on a daily basis?

Come To The Edge

Soulistry Journal Prompt ... traditionally accredited to Guillaume Apollinaire

"Come to the edge" he said.
They said, "We are afraid."
"Come to the edge," he said.
They came. He pushed. They flew.

Soulistry Soul-Questions

* Reflect on a time when you were invited by someone you trusted to *"come to the edge"* (explore possibilities). In your Soulistry Journal, describe the situation.
* What were your thoughts as you considered the possibilities set before you?
* Were you afraid? Did you *"fly"*?
* If the person was not someone you trusted and they invited you to *"the edge"*, what was your response?
* How important is 'trust' a factor in your relationships with family, friends, God, strangers, work colleagues?
* If you don't trust someone, how close do you let them into your heart? your life?
* If you have had your trust betrayed, what does it take for you to trust that person again?
* How can you develop more trust in others/yourself?

Journey Inward

Soulistry Journal Prompt ... Dag Hammarskjöld
The longest journey is the journey inward.

Soulistry Soul-Questions
* What do you understand to be the meaning of *"the journey inward"*?
* Are there components of the *"journey inward"* you have experienced that you could name for others? What are they?
* Might this Soulistry Journal Prompt be applicable to those who are not connected to a religion? If so, how might those people *"journey inward"*?
* How is this particular Soulistry Journal Prompt expressed in your life?

Being Remembered

Soulistry Journal Prompt ... Mattie Stepanek

I want to be remembered as a poet, a peacemaker, and a philosopher who played.

Used by permission.

Soulistry Soul-Questions

* Thirteen year old Mattie wanted to be remembered as a poet, peacemaker, philosopher. By which three words would you like to be remembered?
* What would you like people to say about you at your funeral or when they gather to celebrate your life?
* What words would you like on your grave?
* What words would you like included in your obituary?
* What legacy would you like to leave behind when you die?
* Mattie found 'play' to be an important aspect of his personhood. How is play a part of your life?

Challenge Your Limits

Soulistry Journal Prompt ... Jerry Dunn
Don't limit your challenges; challenge your limits.

Used by permission.

Soulistry Soul-Questions
* What challenges have you had in your life?
  - physically
  - academically
  - creatively
  - vocationally/work-wise
  - emotionally
  - spiritually
  - relationally
  - artistically
  - other

* As you reflect on these challenges, consider a physical challenge you encountered in your life – hearing, sight, mobility, chronic illness, overall fatigue, something else. Did you *"limit your challenge"*? Did you *"challenge your limit"*?

* What about academic/work challenges ... did you *"limit your challenges"*? Did you *"challenge your limits"*?

* What about emotional challenges ... and relationship challenges ... did you *"limit your challenges"* or *"challenge your limits"*? How did you do whatever you did?

* Are you someone who has limited the challenges life has presented or are you someone who has challenged your limits? How?

* If the former is more applicable to your lifestyle and you'd like to be a person who challenges limits rather than a person who limits challenges, reflect on ways you might become such a person.

Excursions Into Enchantment

Soulistry Journal Prompt ... Thomas Moore

The soul has an absolute, unforgiving need for regular excursions into enchantment. It requires them like the body needs food and the mind needs thought.

Soulistry Soul-Questions

* What is your understanding of *"excursions into enchantment"*?
* Reflect on a time when your soul's *"need for regular excursions into enchantment"* was fulfilled. How did that come about?
* What was the occasion? What were the results?
* How might you provide opportunities for *"regular excursions into enchantment"* to happen in your life?
* If your soul does not have such opportunities, what might result?
* The human being (fusion of body, mind and spirit) has needs of *"food ... thought ... regular excursions into enchantment).* Consider creative ways you might bring more balance into your life on a daily basis as you
  - feed your body
  - provide opportunities for thought
  - nourish your artistic nature
  - nurture your spirituality

Epilogue

You're almost at the end of this book.
But there is one Soul-Question left.
It's a simple one, really.
"Who are you?"

As each of us moves through the up's and down's of daily living, we encounter mountains to climb, valleys to survive, lessons to learn, births to deliver, experiences to live, sufferings to endure, and endings to be completed.

As a result, who we are, changes.

Then, as new lessons, valleys, births, experiences, sufferings, mountains and endings re-surface in new guises, once again we change as we re-discover what it is to hope, to rejoice, to trust, to accept, to love, to forgive, to give thanks for all that has brought us to, through and beyond.

Perhaps the questions *"What do you see through the fog-of-life?"* and *"How can clarity of belief, clarity of relationship, clarity of self-knowing, and clarity of life be mine?"* find their answer in a single word: *BE.* For in the be-ing, there is seeing. And in the seeing, there is knowing.

So, with all that you know about yourself today; with all that you believe, stand for, are committed to and represent, how would you respond to the question:

"Who am I, today?"

Consider writing your response to this last question in your Soulistry Journal and remember to date your response.

Blessings to you on your journey. May the path be one of continual learning, challenge, delight, and nourishment. *June*

Appendices

How to Make a Soulistry Journal

Supplies: *leather (or vinyl) piece 6" x 10"; 4 pieces of cardstock 5 ½" x 8 ½"; metal ruler; 2 ½ ft of waxed thread (dental floss works great); needle; scissors; pencil; awl.*

Optional: *embellishments; paper cutter (cuts paper with perfectly straight edge); bone folder (dull-edged device used to crease cardstock/paper in bookbinding and card making).*

Directions

CUT leather (or vinyl) and cardstock to above sizes.

FOLD leather pieces (this is your cover) and cardstock (this is your 'signature')

A 'signature' is a section of sheets in a book/journal

MARK the center of the cardstock and then 1 ½" on each side of the center.

ASSEMBLE by centering cardstock on the inside of the leather cover. Using an awl, make holes at the three marks created in previous step in both cardstock signature and leather cover.

SEW through leather and cardstock at same time
Note: Leaving 3 – 4" thread-tail on outside, pull double thread each time – tight.

a) Thread needle with thread (do not knot at end)
b) From outside, sew through centre hole to inside
c) From inside, sew through one of the other holes
d) From outside, sew back through centre hole again
e) From inside, sew through remaining hole

TO COMPLETE:

- Tie on outside as close as possible to center hole.
- Embellish cover and/or hanging thread with beads/

ribbons etc., if desired.

NOTES:

* The above directions are for a Soulistry Journal with one signature. If you want to have more signatures, repeat above steps.
* Watercolor paper can be used instead of cardstock - great for adding artwork to your Soulistry Journal.
* Thrift stores often have vinyl (good substitute for leather) leather jackets/skirts for sale.
* If you want your Soulistry Journal to be larger, adjust your leather/vinyl cover and cardstock signature according to the size you want.

©june maffin

To view photos of completed Soulistry Journal - set your browser to
http://www.soulistry.com/workshops/journal

Author Biographies

ADDISON, JOSEPH (1672 – 1719) was a British essayist, poet, dramatist, Latin scholar and politician, serving as Under-Secretary of State and Member of Parliament in the Irish House of Commons during the time of the Whig government. His writing skill and friendship with Richard Steele led to the founding of 'The Spectator' magazine.

AMIEL, HENRI (1821 - 1881) was a Swiss philosopher, writer and poet who descended from a Huguenot family. His greatest achievement was the posthumous publication of his journal "Intime" (English translation: Intimate Personal Journal).

APOLLINAIRE, GUILLAUME (1880 - 1918) was a French poet, writer and art critic. Born in Italy (as Wilhelm Albert Włodzimierz Apolinary Kostrowicki), he emigrated at an early age to France where he adopted the name Guillaume Apollinaire. He is credited with coining the word surrealism and making the school of painting called Cubism known. After being wounded in WW1, he died in the Spanish flu pandemic at the early age of thirty eight.

An Aside: Dr. Catherine Moore (Western Illinois University, formerly teaching at Geneva University) has authored several books on Apollinaire. In response to permission to use Apollinaire's quote, Dr. Moore noted that though likely not authored by Apollinaire, the quotation has traditionally been accredited to him.

AUGUSTINE (354 - 430) was a Latin-speaking theologian and philosopher born in present-day Algeria to a pagan father and Roman Catholic mother. After involvement with the Manicheans, he converted to Roman Catholicism, became a bishop, was a key figure in the development of Western Christianity, and was later canonized. He is considered by the Roman Catholic Church and Anglican Communion to be the patron saint of theologians (some say of sore eyes, printers and brewers as well!). Calvinists consider him to be one of the fathers of the Reformation. The Rule of Saint Augustine guides the lives of some Christian monastic orders and men and women living as Augustinians.

BACON, FRANCIS (1909 – 1992) was born in Ireland. While he claimed to be descended from the Elizabethan philosopher with the same name, the life of the self-taught artist Francis Bacon was radically different. His triptych, "Three Studies for Figures at the Base of a Crucifixion" brought him global attention and fame, but not as he might have liked. Rather, it was as an artist who was a bleak chronicler of the human condition. After the death of his partner, his art became preoccupied with death in a unique style: bold, austere, graphic and emotionally raw figurative painting.

BEECHER, HENRY WARD (1813 – 1887) was a social reformer, abolitionist, preacher, speaker and strong advocate of women's suffrage, temperance and Darwin's theory of evolution. His controversial belief that Christianity should adapt itself to the changing culture of the times motivated his strong opposition of slavery and bigotry of any kind: religious, racial, social. His final words are reputed to have been "Now comes the Mystery."

BELL, ALEXANDER GRAHAM (1847 - 1922) began his life in Scotland, first emigrated to Canada and subsequently to the United States where he became an American citizen. Due to the deafness of his parents, he did research on hearing and speech ultimately leading to his invention of the telephone. Coupled with his extraordinary work in hydrofoils and aeronautics, his legacy as one of the founding members of the National Geographic Society left society richer in many ways, not the least of which is a reminder to see the doors open before us.

BLACK, GEMMA is a distinguished Australian calligrapher living in Tasmania whose artistic calligraphic work garners commissions from both the public and private sectors and is a reflection of her love of traditional and contemporary letter forms. Her creative journey has included study of watercolor painting, printmaking and bookbinding and she is renowned as both artist and calligraphic teacher in North America, Europe and Australia. She continues to study, learn and research, be attentive to silence and 'listen.'

http://members.pcug.org.au/~gblack/

BROWN, DENIS is an innovative calligrapher living in Dublin, Ireland. His rigorous formal training in traditional calligraphy and ancient calligraphic traditions combine to form a strong foundation for his experimental work extending calligraphic traditions. Widely traveled, he has lectured on four continents and is internationally recognized in the field of Letter Arts. www.quillskill.com

BUBER, MARTIN (1878 – 1965) was born in Vienna into an Orthodox Jewish family, but broke with Jewish custom to pursue secular studies in philosophy. A cultural Zionist, he was a peacemaker at heart, working to improve the understanding between Israelis and Arabs. With Franz Rosenzweig, he translated the Old Testament into German. He best known for his philosophy of dialogue (centering on the distinction between the I-Thou and I-It relationship), and his retelling of Hasidic tales.

CHIEF SEATTLE (1780 - 1866) was a leader of the Suquamish Native American tribe though not an authentic hereditary chief among Puget Sound Indians. His leadership skills, ability to understand the intentions of white settlers and his reputation as an orator, led to his recognition as a great spiritual leader among his people. A speech arguing in favor of respect for Native American land rites and ecological responsibility has traditionally been accredited to him, though there is no documentation that the words were his.

CHITTISTER, JOAN (b. 1936) has been a Benedictine nun for more than half a century. She is a best-selling author of more than thirty-five books and an international speaker on spirituality, women's issues, human rights, peace and justice. Though she often clashes with Roman Catholic authorities because of her outspoken views on these topics as well as on the ordination of women and the American political scene, her "From Where I Stand" column has a growing readership among people of the Roman Catholic faith as well as people of other faiths. www.benetvision.org/

CHINMOY, SRI (1931 - 2006) was an internationally renowned spiritual teacher, writer, athlete, artist and humanitarian who devoted his life to the pursuit of a dream of a peacefilled world. His philosophy for world peace encouraged people of all backgrounds, faiths and nationalities to work together in this goal. A modern day Renaissance Man, he wrote over 1600 books of prose and poetry, composed nearly 21,000 pieces of music, and performed more than 750 Peace Concerts worldwide, all offered freely. He was an avid runner, tennis player and champion weightlifter. When he died, Nobel Laureates, national leaders of countries around the world, UN officials, religious leaders of all faiths, political figures, humanitarian workers, renowned musicians and world-class athletes from all around the world paid final tributes to this beloved spiritual teacher. www.srichinmoy.org

CONFUCIUS (551 – 479 BCE) was a Chinese philosopher born to a warrior family. His teaching and philosophy deeply influenced Eastern thought and his thoughts developed into a system of philosophy known today as Confucianism. He was a strong proponent of building a harmonious society following the well-known philosophy that people do not do to others what they do not want done to themselves - a very early 'Golden Rule'.

DALAI LAMA (b. 1935) was born with the name Lhamo Dhondup in Tibet. At the age of two, he was recognized as the reincarnation of the 13th Dalai Lama (Dalai Lamas are believed to be manifestations of the Bodhisattva of Compassion - enlightened beings who have chosen to take rebirth in order to serve humanity) and is both the head of state and the spiritual leader of Tibet. The life of His Holiness is guided by three commitments: the promotion of basic human values or secular ethics in the interest of human happiness; the fostering of inter-religious harmony; and the welfare of the Tibetan people. Author of more than seventy books, recipient of over eighty awards including the Nobel Peace Prize for his non-violent struggle for the liberation of Tibet, he became the first Nobel Laureate to be recognized for his concern for global environ-mental issues. His self-description is that of 'a simple Buddhist monk'. www.dalailama.com

D'ANGELO, ANTHONY (b. 1972) is known as the 'devel-opment guru' because of his passionate focus on empowering youth and his one-sentence quips of wisdom. He continues to work toward revolutionizing higher education in his role as Chief Visionary Officer with Collegiate EmPowerment. http://www.collegiate-empowerment.org/core.html

DOZIER, VERNA (1917 - 2006) was a high school English teacher, school administrator, curriculum developer and mentor of countless men and women at the local, national and interna-tional levels of the Episcopal (Anglican) Church. Her ministry was undergirded by a strong belief that laity needed to claim their authority in the world. A story about her speaks of a time when the Diocese of Washington was considering a successor for Bishop John Walker. Citing the historical precedent of Ambrose of Milan, many suggested Verna be nominated. Her reply was reflective of her strong belief in the importance of laity. She responded by saying that at her stage in life, she was not willing to accept a demotion from lay person to bishop.

DUNN, JERRY (b. 1946) is known as America's Marathon Man. Running in hundreds of marathon races in his lifetime, he celebrated his sixtieth birthday by running sixty miles. In his local running store in 1990 talking about his upcoming run across the United States in support of Habit for Humanity, a salesperson said that Jerry was one of those people who doesn't limit their challenges but challenge their limits. Jerry has been signing and living his life that way ever since. www.leanhorse.com

DUSE, ELEANORA (1858 - 1924) was an Italian actress whose family situation necessitated her working in an acting troupe from the age of four. Quiet, introverted and private, she was a strong influence to many artists including poet Amy Lowell and dancer Martha Graham. Her love of simple things in life brought her "soul-alive" in spite of having endured the loss of a child and ill health for most of her adult life.

EMERSON, RALPH WALDO (1803 - 1882) was a prolific essayist, philosopher and poet. He made his living as an educator, was ordained as a Unitarian minister following in his father's footsteps, but resigned four years later after a dispute with church authorities. Emerson's contribution to the world of writing lies in his elaborately indexed journal-keeping which he began while at Harvard University.

FRANCIS OF ASSISI (1182 – 1226) is honored by many Christians as the patron saint of animals as well as the patron saint of ecology. When blindness limited his life, he wrote the Canticle of Brother Sun that showed his love of creation. Born to wealth, his life emphasized and reflected a life of simplicity and poverty. Many followed him and in time, Roman Catholic and Anglican religious orders were established which follow the rule of St. Francis, known today as the Franciscan Order.

FREUD, SIGMUND (1856 – 1939) was an Austrian neurologist who developed the psychoanalytic method of psychiatry. His work in the relevance of dreams remains seminal in the human quest for self-awareness and understanding. www.freudfile.org

FROST, ROBERT (1874 – 1963) was a highly regarded American poet whose poetry represented rural life and American colloquial speech of the early 1900's. Frost received four Pulitzer Prizes for Poetry in his lifetime – a most unusual honor. www.frostfriends.org

GABIROL, SOLOMON IBN (c. 1021 – 1058) aka Solomon ben Judah was a Jewish philosopher and poet. At the age of twenty, he wrote "Anak," a versified acrostic consisting of four hundred verses divided into ten parts.

GANDHI, MAHATMA (1869 - 1948) was born Mohandas Karamchand Gandhi in India where he became a political and spiritual leader and is officially honored as the Father of the Nation. He pioneered satyagraha, a philosophy founded upon ahimsa or total nonviolence; worked to help India gain its independence from the British Commonwealth; and inspired people and movements for civil rights and freedom across the world. A member of India's National Congress, Mahatma (means Great Soul) led nationwide campaigns to ease poverty, expand women's rights, build religious and ethnic amity, end untoucha-bility, and increase economic self-reliance. www.mahatma.com/

GAUTAMA, SIDDHĀRTHA (563 – 483 BC) was known as Buddha (meaning 'enlightened/awakened one'). He was a spiritual teacher from India whose legacy to the world is the religious philosophy of Buddhism. Various collections of his teachings were passed down by oral tradition (the first writing of those teachings about 400 years after his death) and now comprise Buddhist scripture.

GIBRAN, KAHLIL (1883 - 1931) was born in modern-day Lebanon. With his family, he emigrated to the United States, where he began his literary career, studied art and wrote his inspirational book, "The Prophet" which became so popular that he is reputed to be the third best-selling poet of all time after Shakespeare and Lao Tzu.

GUENTHER, MARGARET (b. 1929) is an Episcopal priest, spiritual director, noted author and lay medical practitioner. She is Professor Emerita of Ascetical Theology at General Theological Seminary where she also served for many years as

Director of the Center for Christian Spirituality.

HAMMARSKJÖLD, DAG (1905 – 1961) has been described as a Renaissance man linguist, athlete (mountaineer, skier, gymnast), theologian and Swedish diplomat. He was equally comfortable discussing poetry as he was discussing French Impressionistic painting and classical music. He served the United Nations as Secretary-General for two five-year terms. After his death, the publication of 'Markings', his spiritual diary revealed his spiritual journey over the years. www.dhf.uu.se/

HANCOCK, ALICE is a creative calligrapher and designer; owner of RED (Real Exceptional Design); and creator of Greentherapie – an innovative, alternative and holistic 'outside-the-box' therapy to help those living with cancer be empowered with knowledge and resources to live life fully. www.green-therapie.com

HANH, THICH NHAT (b. 1926) has been a Vietnamese Buddhist monk since he was sixteen. Working tirelessly for reconciliation between North and South Vietnam, his lifelong efforts to generate peace moved Martin Luther King Jr. to nominate him for the Nobel Peace Prize. Living in exile in France (where he founded a retreat centre), he is a prolific writer, renowned scholar, world leader and spiritual guide, championing a movement that weaves traditional meditative practices with nonviolent civil disobedience. His teachings revolve around respect for life, generosity, loving communication, and cultivation of a healthy lifestyle. His Mindfulness meditation technique continues to help people in their desire for wholeness and inner calm. www.plumvillage.org

HARJO, JOY (b. 1951) is an American poet, social activist, university professor, screenplay writer, author and member of Poetic Justice, a band that combines music with poetry. She was born in Oklahoma into a family of Muscogee (Creek) painters and is of Cherokee descent. She has received many awards for her various writings notably the Lifetime Achievement

Award from the Native Writers Circle of the Americas. www.joyharjo.com

HEARD, GERALD (1889 - 1971) was a historian, science writer, educator, author and philosopher as well as mentor to numerous people including Clare Booth Luce and Bill Wilson, the co-founder of Alcoholics Anonymous. Heard founded Trabuco College in California as a facility for the study of comparative religion studies and termed the phase 'Leptoid Man' (from the Greek word lepsis: "to leap") to describe his hope for the future development of the human race: a human being of developed spirituality. www.geraldheard.com

HUGHES, LANGSTON (1902 – 1967) was a Harlem poet and essayist who began writing poetry in grade eight. A prolific writer, drawing from the literary genius of Carl Sandberg and Walt Whitman, he devoted his life to lecturing and writing novels, poetry, short story collections, plays, musicals, operas, radio and television scripts. He was a member of an abolitionist family and his insightful and colorful works gave voice to the Black experience in America. His New York City home street block of East 127th was renamed Langston Hughes Place in his honor.

JACKSON, JILL (1913 - 1995) realized the presence of a Higher Power in her life after recovering from a suicide attempt and its resultant paralysis. She found a deep faith and received the inspiration for the words to the song 'Let there be Peace on Earth'. The focus for the rest of her life was to encourage the personal responsibility of each person in creating peace in the world. Out of her tragic situation came a life of empowerment for her and inspiration for many.

JESUS OF NAZARETH (c. 5 BCE – c. 30 CE), also known as Jesus Christ, was born into the Jewish faith. For over 2000 years, many religions have regarded him as a teacher and healer. Christians (followers of a religion based on the life of Jesus, the principal of 'love of neighbor' and personal transformation) believe him to be the long-awaited Messiah.

JULIAN OF NORWICH (1342 – 1416) was an English mystic about whom little is known. Her writings represent an abiding love of God, an attitude of joy rather than the negative view at the time in history (likely due to the Black Death and peasant revolts) and a theological belief in a connection between God and motherhood. An early feminist!

KÜBLER-ROSS, ELISABETH (1926 - 2004) was a mother, scientist, physician, educator, psychiatrist, and author of "On Death and Dying" among countless other works. She was inducted into the National Women's Hall of Fame, recipient of over twenty honorary degrees and strong advocate of the Hospice care movement. www.ekrfoundation.org

LAO TZU (c. 4th or 6th century B.C.E.) was a wise Chinese philosopher, supposedly the author of many quotes and credited with being the founder of Taoism. Many legends revolve around his conception, birth, life and longevity thus any biographical statement would be conjecture.

LARS is a blogger, philosopher and writer. While granting permission to use this quote as a Soulistry Journal Prompt, Lars requested anonymity, thus no biographical information is provided.

LIGHT, GORDON is a retired bishop in the Anglican Church of Canada and a founding member of the music group known as the Common Cup Company. The words of the 'Draw the Circle Wide' Soulistry Journal Prompt are the chorus of a hymn he wrote by the same name which became the theme for the Anglican Church of Canada's triennial gathering of their 2007 General Synod. www.commoncup.com

L'ENGLE, MADELEINE (1918 - 2007) was a prolific American writer whose numerous novels reflect an eclectic interest in life. A woman of deep faith, her deep questioning influenced her belief in God and resulted in many of her books reflecting the belief that religion, science and magic are merely different aspects of a single reality which originate from God/Higher Power/Creator. www.madeleinelengle.com

MAATHAI, WANGARI (b. 1940) is an environmental and political activist who was born in Kenya. She received the Nobel Peace Prize for her contribution to sustainable development, democracy and peace; was an elected Member of Parliament; founded the Greenbelt Movement which has planted over thirty million trees in Kenya to help prevent soil erosion; and was awarded the first PhD by the University of Nairobi. She became Visiting Fellow at Yale University's Global Institute of Sustainable Forestry and has been increasingly active on both environmental and women's issues. Her husband divorced her, reputedly saying that she was too strong-minded for a woman and that he was unable to control her. After the judge in the divorce case agreed with her husband (!), she was put in jail for speaking out against the judge who then decreed that she could no longer use her husband's surname. In defiance, she chose to add an extra "a" to her last name - changing, but not changing it. She has experienced imprisonment and physical attack for demanding multi-party elections and an end to tribal politics and political corruption in Kenya. www.greenbelt-movement.org

MANSFIELD, KATHERINE (1888 – 1923) was born Kathleen Mansfield Beauchamp in New Zealand and adopted the pen name of Katherine Mansfield. The repression of the Maori people drew her away from NZ to Great Britain when she was only twenty years old where she became a prominent and prolific modernist writer of short fiction likely due in large part to her friendship with writers such as D.H. Lawrence and Virginia Woolf. Journaling was a significant part of her life. A street in Menton, France, where she lived and wrote, is named after her; a Fellowship in her name is offered annually to a New Zealand writer; and New Zealand's pre-eminent short story competition is named in her honor.

MEISTER ECKHART (1260 – c. 1327) was born Eckhart von Hochheim but was commonly known as Meister (German for 'master' referring to the academic title he received). German theologian and philosopher, he is considered to be one of the great mystics in history and one of the most influential Christian Neoplatonists of the Middle Ages. His unorthodox teachings made him suspect to the Roman Catholic Church. Tried for heresy in the final years of his life by Pope John XXII, reportedly he died before the results of his trial were announced.

MERTON, THOMAS (1915 - 1968) was a monk, poet, spiritual writer, social activist and proponent of inter-religious dialogue that led to meetings with the Dalai Lama and Thich Nhat Hanh. A prolific writer, he was influenced by the writings and life stories of poets William Blake and Gerard Manley Hopkins. He speaks to the hearts and minds of those searching for answers to life's questions - which he believed was the essence of spirituality. While Merton struggles with how one can be contemplative in a world of action, his faith leads him to conclude that God must be discovered as the centre of one's being. www.merton.org

MICHELANGELO (1475 - 1564) was a sculptor, poet, Renaissance painter, architect and engineer whose reputation has endured for centuries. His paintings in the Sistine Chapel in Rome, his architectural use of pilasters, sculptures of the Pieta and the David (before he was 30!) are just some examples of his artistic brilliance. Not as well known for his words, they too remain examples of his creative spirituality long after his death.

MOORE, THOMAS (1779 – 1852) was a songwriter, translator, novelist, biographer, balladeer, literary executor to Lord Byron and considered to be Ireland's National Bard (poet).

NAGARJUNA (c. 150 - 250 CE) Little is known about his life, though legends abound. Some documents state that he was born to an upper-cast Brahmin family in Southern India and later converted to Buddhism. His contributions to Buddhist philosophy are reported to be the concept of "emptiness" and the development of the two-truths doctrine. In the Jodo Shinshu branch of Buddhism, Nagarjuna is considered the First Patriarch.

NIN, ANAÏS (1903 - 1977) was a French author who became famous for her journals which she began writing when she was eleven years old and continued until shortly before she died. According to her journals, she trained as a flamenco dancer in Paris, modeled in New York City and was intimately acquainted with a number of well-known figures of the time including Henry Miller. www.anaisnin.com

O'DRISCOLL, HERBERT is an Anglican priest who was born in Ireland and now lives on Vancouver Island in Canada. Celebrated scholar and author of many books on the spiritual life, lyrics to the hymns he has written have found their way into innumerable hymn books. Internationally known for his preaching genius, story telling and creative thinking this former Dean of the College of Preachers in Washington, D.C. continues to be a sought-after speaker in his retirement.

OVERTON, PATRICK is an educator, author, lyricist, keynote speaker, poet and visual artist. Formerly Associate Professor of Communication and Cultural Studies at Columbia College in Missouri, Dr. Overton is now the Director of the Front Porch Institute in Astoria, Oregon and an ordained minister in the Christian Church (Disciples of Christ). www.patrick-overton.com

REDMOON, AMBROSE (1933 - 1996) was the pseudonym of James Neil Hollingworth. He was an American writer and manager of the rock band Quicksilver Messenger Service and spent the last thirty years of his life as a paraplegic as a result of a car accident. A man of strong faith, his life was a testimony to his courage.

RILKE, RAINER MARIA (1875 - 1926) was born in Prague in the Czech Republic. On a visit to Russia, he was deeply impressed by what he learned of Russian mysticism and began writing 'The Book of Hours: The Book of Monastic Life' which expressed his spiritual yearning.

ROOSEVELT, ANNA ELEANOR (1884 - 1962) won international respect and admiration in her role as First Lady of the United States to her husband, Franklin D. Roosevelt. Concern for humanity made her the driving force behind the Universal Declaration of Human Rights, the primary international agreement among nations as to the fundamental and inalienable rights and freedoms of all human beings. Confronting both opportunity and adversity with a sense of optimism and determination, she was a tireless worker whose humility, common sense approach, sense of humor and constant optimism contributed to her reputation as one of the most admired people of the twentieth century. www.rooseveltinstitute.org/

SCHWEITZER, ALBERT (1875 - 1965) was recognized as an international concert organist. This provided him with a much-needed income to pay for his medical schooling and the hospital he founded. Linguist that he was, his published works were in English, French and German. After release from a French internment camp, he expanded his hospital in Lambaréné to seventy buildings where he served in a variety of roles: surgeon, pastor, village administrator, building and grounds superintendent, writer, contemporary history commentator, musician, and gracious host to countless visitors. Recipient of the Nobel Peace Prize, he started a leprosarium with the monies he received. He was buried at his beloved Lambaréné. www.albertschweitzer.com

SEXTON, ANNE (1928 - 1974) was born Anne Gray Harvey. In response to her lifelong battle with Bipolar Disorder, she resorted to writing poetry as part of her healing journey. Soon after connecting with her creative nature creative part she was able to make her living as an American poet and writer. A collaboration with musicians resulted in the formation of a group (known as Anne Sexton and Her Kind) that put music to her words.

STARR, PAMELA VAULL (1909 - 1993) was also known as Violet Isabelle Carter Popp. She was a gifted American poet, artist, and writer whose social service (notably the Girl Scouts and American Red Cross) was a vital part of her life. She was instrumental in the founding of the Idyllwild branch of the National League of American Pen Women – a community of professional artists, writers, poets, composers, and arrangers which believes in the power of words, art, and music to illuminate the human experience, fire the imagination, and nurture the soul. www.americanpenwomen.org

STEPANEK, MATTIE (1991 - 2004) was only thirteen years old when he died of a rare neuromuscular disease; but in that time, he became a best-selling author, poet, philosopher, theologian, peace activist and philanthropist. The Muscular Dystrophy Mattie Fund has been established in his memory to help find treatments and cures for childhood neuromuscular diseases. His poetry explores disability, despair and death, but also reflects on the gifts he finds in prayer, peace, nature and his belief in something "bigger and better than the here and now". His funeral eulogy was delivered by former American President Jimmy Carter who said that for all his youth, Mattie's philosophy on peace helped shape his own philosophy and that Mattie was the "most extraordinary person I have met in my life." www.mattieonline.com

TEILLARD DE CHARDIN, PIERRE (1881 - 1955) was a Christian mystic of many interests and gifts. He became a Jesuit priest, trained as a paleontologist and was a writer whose book "The Phenomenon of Man" (sic) abandoned traditional religious interpretations of creation as set forth in the Bible's book of Genesis which led to its publication ban during his lifetime by Pope John XXIII. www.teilharddechardin.org

THOREAU, HENRY DAVID (1817 - 1863) was an American poet, naturalist, author, transcendentalist, historian and philosopher. As well, he was a lifelong abolitionist whose philosophy of civil disobedience (improving, not abolishing government) influenced Mahatma Gandhi and Martin Luther King Jr.

THORNTON, PETER was born in England and now resides in the United States. A full-time professional calligrapher and artist for over forty years, he is a Fellow of the Calligraphy and Lettering Arts Society (C.L.A.S.) with an international reputation as a gifted teacher and calligrapher. His lighthearted wit and playful approach to teaching brings students eager to learn from him in workshops he has offered throughout the world. He has authored several books including *Alphabetically Speaking*, co-curated a book that showcases the work of Adolf Bernd's calligraphy and has become known for his exploration of the visually and acoustically exciting world of "musicalligraphy" - a combination of sound and letters.

TOURNIER, PAUL (1898 - 1986) was a Swiss author and physician who was active in the World Council of Churches. His work in pastoral counseling had a profound impact on his deep belief that human beings are more than just a body and a mind. He believed that people are also spiritual beings and health care must address this in overall patient care.

TUTU, DESMOND MPILO (b. 1931) is a noted author, cleric and recipient of numerous awards including the Nobel Peace Prize, the Albert Schweitzer Prize for Humanitarianism, and the Gandhi Peace Prize. He was the first black South African Anglican Archbishop of South Africa, as well as Primate of the Church of the Anglican Church of Southern Africa. His activism is evidenced in his campaigns against AIDS, tuberculosis, homophobia, poverty and racism and his opposition of apartheid brought worldwide recognition. Many perceive him to be South Africa's moral conscience, the voice of the voiceless. www.tutu.org

TWAIN, MARK (1835 - 1910) is the pen name for Samuel

Langhorne Clemens. American author and satirist, he was friend to politicians, artists, industrialists and royalty. Praised by both critics and peers, on his death he was lauded as the greatest American humorist of his age.

UNAMUNO, MIGUEL DE (1864 – 1936) was a Spanish essayist, novelist, philosopher, playwright, author, educator, academic, linguist (14 languages) and poet. Dr. Unamuno experienced a crisis of faith leading to his conclusion that insofar as there is no rational explanation of God, one must abandon all pretense of rationalism and embrace faith. A strong opponent of Marxism, his faith came to be important during periods of political arrest.

WAKEFIELD, DAN is an American author whose 'Spiritual Autobiography' and 'Creating from the Spirit' workshops have encouraged agnostics, atheists and people of faith in their spiritual journeying. www.danwakefield.com

WEAVER, GWEN is a highly creative American calligrapher and teacher whose joy of shell gathering and hieroglyphs remains with her today. Living in Turkey for two years brought her to European museums and art galleries which resulted in the selection of Art History as her University major. Later, the art of drafting and machine design kept her employed and fascinated for decades. While trained in the broad edged pen, it was the pointed pen that brought Gwen to a wondrous love and the creation of her delightful and unique Weaver Writing. www.pointedpen.com

WESLEY, JOHN (1703 – 1791) was a priest in the Church of England who, with his brother Charles, created a discussion group that focused on holy living, charity and theological inquiry and were known as the founders of Methodism. In spite of opposition, he was among the first to preach for the rights of slaves. Renowned for his preaching, publishing, hymnody and writing skills, Wesley's life represents an amazing account of service and tireless holy living.

WILCOX, ELLA WHEELER (1851 - 1919) was a prolific American writer of prose and poetry. Her strength was her belief in the triumph of hope over despair, of victory over failure, of good over evil, and of kindness over selfishness. She believed that the harshness of life was an opportunity to change lead into gold. She deeply appreciated the need for and the beauty of diverse religious faiths.

AND

CHEROKEE LEGENDS have been passed down from generation to generation. The Cherokee believe in one Supreme Being who nurtures their intention of living in harmony with their natural environment. The purpose of the Cherokee Legends is to teach life's important lessons to the children so that in turn, they would share the lessons with their children.

CHINESE PROVERBS are usually short and memorable sayings that have stood the test of time. They are inspirational, motivational and are often filled with words of wisdom.

NAVAJO CHANTS often speak of the gifts of Mother Earth, believing that when there is balance/connection with Mother Earth, a sense of well-being and happiness are manifested. The Navajo traditionally call themselves the Diné. They are semi-autonomous and live on the largest land area assigned to a United States Native American jurisdiction - parts of Arizona, New Mexico and Utah.

SANSKRIT PROVERBS Sanskrit is one of twenty-two official languages of today's India. Its origins were in ancient times as early as 1700 BCE. Sanskrit writing is multi-dimensional: poetic, dramatic, philosophical, religious as well as scientific and technical texts and has been widely used as a ceremonial language in the form of hymns and mantras in Hinduism, Buddhism and sometimes in Jainism. Sanskrit writings are noted to be wonderful repositories of wisdom.

Soulistry Journal Prompt Titles

Aging ... Mark Twain

"Age is an issue of mind over matter. If you don't mind, it doesn't matter."

Aiming High ... Michelangelo

"The greatest danger for most of us is not that our aim is too high and we miss it, but that it is too low and we reach it."

All Shall Be Well ... Julian of Norwich

"All shall be well. All shall be well. And all manner of things shall be well."

And the Day Came ... Anaïs Nin

"And the day came when the risk to remain tight in the bud was more painful than the risk it took to blossom."

A Spiritual Experience ... Pierre Teillard de Chardin

"We are not human beings having a spiritual experience. We are spiritual beings having a human experience."

A Spirituality of Play ... Margaret Guenther

"When we play, we also celebrate holy uselessness. Like the calf frolicking in the meadow, we need no pretense or excuses. Work is productive; play, in its disinterestedness and self-forgetting, can be fruitful. When we forget to play, we've forgotten the joy of creation."

A Spirituality of Work ... Confucius

"If you enjoy what you do, you'll never work another day in your life."

Being Remembered ... Mattie Stepanek

"I want to be remembered as a poet, a peacemaker, and a philosopher who played."

Believing ... Verna Dozier

"What difference does it make that you believe?"

Blessed Are You ... Jesus of Nazareth

"Blessed are the peacemakers for they shall be called the children of God".

Challenge Your Limits ... traditionally accredited to Jerry Dunn

"Don't limit your challenges; challenge your limits."

Come to the Edge ... Guillaume Apollinaire

"Come to the edge" he said. They said "We are afraid." "Come to the edge" he said. They came. He pushed. They flew."

Courage ... Ambrose Redmoon

"Courage is not the absence of fear, but rather the judgment that something else is more important than fear."

Darkness Deserves Gratitude ... Joan Chittister

"Darkness deserves gratitude. It is the alleluia point at which we learn to understand that all growth does not take place in the sunlight."

Deepening the Mystery ... Francis Bacon

"The job of the artist is always to deepen the mystery."

Doing Good ... John Wesley

"Do all the good you can, by all the means you can, in all the ways you can, in all the places you can, at all the times you can, to all the people you can, as long as ever you can."

Doing What You Think You Cannot Do ... Eleanor Roosevelt

"You gain strength, courage and confidence by every experience in which you really stop to look fear in the face. You must do the thing which you think you cannot do."

Draw the Circle Wide ... Gordon Light

"Draw the circle wide, draw it wider still.
Let this be our song – no one stands alone, standing side by side."

Excursions to Enchantment ... Thomas Moore

"The soul has an absolute, unforgiving need for regular excursions into enchantment. It requires them like the body needs food and the mind needs thought."

Faith ... Patrick Overton

"When you walk to the edge of all the light you have
and take that first step into the darkness of the unknown,
you must believe that one of two things will happen:
There will be something solid for you to stand upon,

Or, you will be taught how to fly."

Feeding the Wolf ... Cherokee legend

A Cherokee elder sitting with his grandchildren told them this story. "In everyone's life, there is a terrible daily fight — a fight between two wolves. One wolf is evil - this one is negativity, fear, anger, envy, greed, arrogance, self-pity, resentment, frustration, boredom and deceit. The other wolf is good - this one is joy, serenity, self-control, humility, goodness, confidence, generosity, truth, kindness, gentleness, love, patience and compassion". A child asked, "Grandfather, which wolf wins the fight"? The elder looked him in the eye. "The one you feed."

Finding God's Presence ... Herbert O'Driscoll

"Come and journey, journey upward. Sing God's praises, offer prayer.

In the storm and in the stillness, find God's presence everywhere."

Forgiveness ... Mahatma Gandhi

"If we practice an eye for an eye and a tooth for a tooth, soon the whole world will be blind and toothless."

Friends Near and Far Away ... Kahlil Gibran

"A friend who is far away is sometimes much nearer than one who is at hand. Is not the mountain far more awe-inspiring and more clearly visible to one passing through the valley than to those who inhabit the mountain?"

Gift ... Denis Brown

"Everybody has a gift. Your job is to find it, love it, nourish it and give it space to grow. It's not too late for anyone to commit to making space for their own nature to blossom."

Gladdening The Hearts ... Henri Amiel

"Life is short and we do not have much time to gladden the hearts of those who travel the way with us. So, be swift to love and make haste to be kind."

God's Milk ... Anne Sexton

"There is hope. There is hope everywhere. Today God gives milk,

and I have the pail."

Gratitude ... Meister Eckhart

"If the only prayer you say is thank you, that would suffice."

Happiness ... Chinese Proverb

"If you want happiness for an hour, take a nap. If you want happiness for a day, go fishing. If you want happiness for a lifetime, help someone else."

Hatred Ceases ... Siddhärtha Gautama (Buddha)

"Hatred does not cease through hatred at any time. Hatred ceases through love."

Holding Fast to Dreams ... Langston Hughes

"Hold fast to dreams, for if dreams die, life is a broken winged bird that cannot fly."

Hope Has Two Daughters ... Augustine

"Hope has two daughters. Their names are anger and courage; anger at the way things are and courage to see that they do not remain the way they are."

Journey Inward ... Dag Hammarskjöld

"The longest journey is the journey inward."

Keening ... Lars

"Suffering lost in itself, the song lost in the song: keening sounds over the plain."

Keeping Secrets ... Paul Tournier

"Nothing makes us so lonely as our secrets."

Laughing at Ourselves ... Katherine Mansfield

"When we can begin to take our failures seriously, it means we are ceasing to be afraid of them. It is of immense importance to learn to laugh at ourselves."

Life Goes On ... Robert Frost

"In three words, I can sum up everything I've learned about life. It goes on."

Light From Within ... Elisabeth Kübler-Ross

"People are like stained-glass windows. They sparkle and shine when the sun is out, but when the darkness sets in, their true beauty

is revealed only if there is a light from within."

Living Life With Confidence ... Henry David Thoreau

"Go confidently in the direction of your dreams. Live the life you've imagined. "

Look Well To This Day ... Sanskrit Proverb

"Yesterday is but a dream and tomorrow is only a vision. But today, well lived makes every yesterday a dream of happiness and every tomorrow a vision of hope. Look well, therefore, to this day."

Loving Your Enemy ... Jesus of Nazareth

"Love your enemies. If you love only those who love you, what good is that? If you are kind only to your friends, how are you different from anyone else?"

May I Walk ... Navajo Chants

"Happily may I walk. Happily, with abundant dark clouds, may I walk. Happily, with abundant showers, may I walk. Happily, with abundant plants, may I walk. Happily, on a trail of pollen, may I walk. With beauty before me, may I walk. With beauty behind me, may I walk. With beauty above me may I walk. With beauty below me may I walk. With beauty all around me, may I walk. Wandering on a trail of beauty, lively I walk."

May You Be Blessed ... St. Francis of Assisi

"May you be blessed with discomfort at easy answers, half truths and superficial relationships so that you may live deep within your heart. May you be blessed with anger at injustice, oppression and exploitation of people so that you may work for justice, freedom and peace. May you be blessed with tears to shed for those who suffer pain, rejection, hunger and war so that you may reach out your hand to comfort them and turn their pain into joy. And may you be blessed with enough foolishness to believe that you can make a difference in the world so that you can do what others claim cannot be done to bring justice and kindness to all children and the poor."

Mystery ... Martin Buber

"Real faith means holding ourselves open to the unconditional

mystery which we encounter in every sphere of our life."

Nothing You Can Do ... Desmond Tutu

"There is nothing you can do that will make God love you more, there is nothing you can do that will make God love you less."

Open Doors ... Alexander Graham Bell

"When one door closes another door opens; but we often look so long and so regretfully upon the closed door, that we do not see the ones which open for us."

Peace Within ... Jill Jackson

"Let there be peace on earth and let it begin with me. Let there be peace on earth, the peace that was meant to be. With God our Creator, family all are we. (alternate sentence: With Earth as our Mother, her children all are we) *Let us walk with each other, in perfect harmony. Let peace begin with me, let this be the moment now. With every step I take let this be my solemn vow: to take each moment and live each moment in peace eternally. Let there be peace on earth and let it begin with me."*

Problem-Solving ... Anthony D'Angelo

"When solving problems, dig at the roots instead of just hacking at the leaves."

Questions that Speak ... Chinese Proverb

"Those who ask questions may be fools for five minutes; but those who do not ask remain fools forever."

Radiating Intrinsic Goodness ... Wangari Maathai

"We can work together for a better world with men and women of goodwill, those who radiate the intrinsic goodness of humankind."

Rekindling the Light ... Albert Schweitzer

"Sometimes our light goes out, but is blown into flame by another human being. Each of us owes deepest thanks to those who have rekindled this light."

Religious Belief ... Dalai Lama

"My religion is very simple. My religion is kindness. Practice kindness whenever it is possible. It is always possible."

Rising Every Time ... Confucius

"Our greatest glory is not in never falling, but in rising every time

we fall."

Risking Frustration ... Thomas Merton

"To hope is to risk frustration. Therefore, make up your mind to risk frustration."

Secret of the Spiritual Life ... Gerald Heard

"The whole secret of the spiritual life is just this painful struggle to come awake, to become really conscious."

Seeing the Spirit Sparkle ... Gwen Weaver

"Are any of us perfect? I don't think so. I would rather like to see the spirit. It's the sparkle in the eye - the slight opening of the soul."

Six Letters ... Gemma Black

"Silent - Listen: Six letters. Two words. One meaning"

Soul-Alive ... Eleonora Duse

"If the sight of the blue skies fills you with joy; if a blade of grass springing up in the fields has power to move you; if the simple things of nature have a message that you understand, rejoice, for your soul is alive!"

Soul-Harvest ... Lao Tzu

"Nurturing your love is like tending a small garden. If you keep pulling up the plants to see if the roots are growing, you will not harvest anything."

Soul-Stars ... Pamela Vaull Starr

"Reach high, for stars lie hidden in your soul. Dream deep, for every dream precedes the goal."

Spiritual Mountain-Climbing ... Sri Chinmoy

"Spirituality is constant inner mountain-climbing."

Success ... Henry Ward Beecher

"One's best success comes after their greatest disappointments."

The Acquisition of Wisdom ... Solomon ibn Gabirol

"The first step in the acquisition of wisdom is silence; the second listening; the third, memory; the fourth, practice; the fifth, teaching others."

The Art of Being Kind ... Ella Wheeler Wilcox

"So many gods, so many creeds, so many paths that wind and wind

while just the art of being kind is all the sad world needs."

The Idea of God ... traditionally attributed to **Madeleine L'Engle,** likely authored by **Miguel de Unamuno**

"Those who believe that they believe in God, but without passion in their hearts, without anguish of mind, without uncertainty, without doubt, without an element of despair even in their consolation, believe only in the God idea, not God."

The Mark of Wisdom ... **Ralph Waldo Emerson**

"The invariable mark of wisdom is to see the miraculous in the common."

The Only Journey ... **Rainer Maria Rilke**

"The only journey is the one within."

The Web of Life ... traditionally attributed to **Chief Seattle**

"Humankind has not woven the web of life. We are but one thread within it. Whatever we do to the web, we do to ourselves. All things are bound together. All things connect."

The Well Within ... **Thich Nhat Hanh**

"The well is within us. If we dig deeply in the present moment, the water will spring forth."

Today I Am Asking ... **Alice Hancock**

"Today I am asking you to help one, to cheer one, to give hope to one ... yourself."

Today's Road ... traditionally attributed to **Nagarjuna**

"I always knew that one day I would take this road, but yesterday I did not know today would be the day."

Tomorrow's Seeds ... **Chinese Proverb**

"All the flowers of all the tomorrows are in the seeds of today."

Trusting the Unseen ... **Ralph Waldo Emerson**

"All I have seen teaches me to trust the Creator for all I have not seen."

Vulnerability ... **Sigmund Freud**

"Out of your vulnerabilities will come your strength."

Walking In and Out ... **Joy Harjo**

"I walk in and out of many worlds."

What Does Love Look Like ... Augustine

"What does love look like? It has the hands to help others. It has the feet to hasten to the poor and needy. It has eyes to see misery and want. It has the ears to hear the sighs and sorrows. This is what love looks like."

What is Spirituality ... Dan Wakefield

"Spirituality emerges not in religious terms, but in care for friends and fellow human beings, in the passion for learning and perfecting one's craft, for enjoying and appreciating the commonplace gifts of everyday experience and finding in them the inspiration for living more fully."

What We See ... Peter Thornton

"When you look at your neighbor's work, you see it for what it is. When you look at your own work, you see it for what it isn't."

Worldly Inexperience ... Joseph Addison

"Prejudice and self-sufficiency naturally proceed from inexperience of the world and ignorance."

The Soulistry Story

"It's grace, pure and simple."

That's what I tell people when they ask about Soulistry.

The Soulistry story began early in 2004 when mercury poisoning resulted in the atrophying of my muscles (legs, arms, voice) along with sleepless nights and long days of exhaustion filled with pain. I wasn't able to read, think clearly, find solace in books, enjoy visits or even conversations with family and friends.

Unable to sleep one night, I found myself looking at the top shelf of my office closet where I'd stored a variety of things. Before I knew it, I had taken a plain, wooden framed mirror and started adding a variety of embellishments. I continued to play and create, and the pain seemed to lessen. Eventually, I was able to sleep. In the morning, I saw the mirror and was struck by its beauty and simplicity.

I sensed that some new thing was happening. I could feel my spirit soaring. A part of my brain was working - my right brain! I began to wonder: *"If I focus on activating my right brain, could my left brain possibly begin to work again?"* In a moment of prayer – a conversation with the Creator, I clearly heard affirmation, encouragement and hope: *"Develop your right brain. Healing will come"*.

How was I supposed to do that? While creativity had been expressed in my life in various ways, I'd never thought of myself as 'artistic'. But, as I began to experiment with cardstock, paper, pen and ink, watercolors and the mirrors, I came to realize that I **was** artistic. The more I played and created, the more my right brain activity increased and the more aware I was that my left brain was becoming more active … letters finally formed into words - I could read again! I began to think with clarity and enter into conversations and visits with family and friends.

The combination of two words (soul + artistry) into one new word *"Soulistry"* became the umbrella for the Meditation Mirrors, handmade cards and bookmarks that began to find their way into art shows and Christmas fairs. And, they were selling!

My soul was being nourished through a variety of artistic expressions. I began to think of myself as an artist and coined a phrase - Creative Spirituality Artist.

I began to realize that the next step in my healing was to 'step out in faith' ... combine my experiences as an educator, Creative Spirituality Artist, writer and spiritual director/soul friend. And that's how the Soulistry Workshops and Retreats were born. Out of a devastating medical crisis where the future looked bleak, new life emerged in ways I had never even imagined.

Word began to spread and invitations to speak at conferences and facilitate Soulistry workshops and retreats in various places throughout North America and Europe continue to come my way. I love to travel and encourage people in their self-growth/spiritual development, so each invitation is greeted with much joy and anticipation as possibilities are considered. This journey is very humbling – and exciting!

Along the way, the idea for a new book (ABC Publishing published my spiritual autobiography *"Disturbed by God: A Journey of Spiritual Discovery"* now out of print, but available as an e-book at http://www.soulistry.com/ Soulistry/E-Book.html) slowly began to surface. I began to collect quotations, research authorship, write mini author biographies, contact authors/their representatives requesting permission to use their quotation and created accompanying Soul-Questions. It was a project that kept my brain active and helped to move the heavy metal toxicity out of my body. And, on top of all of that, it was fun!

One day, I received an unexpected email from the publisher of Circle Books asking if my work might fit into their new imprint line. I wondered, "Might the publication of the book be the next step for Soulistry?"

After several emails back and forth, it seemed that publication of the book really was the next step. And, *Soulistry* is now a book and an e-book!

Yes – Soulistry's story is a story of *grace … pure and simple.*

Soulistry retreats and workshops

Created to encourage the living of a balanced life with purpose, joy and inner peace and exploration of the connection between creativity and spirituality (art and soul), each Soulistry Workshop and Retreat is designed to offer opportunities for participants to re-awaken their creativity, release their playful nature, and deepen their spirituality in unique ways. No previous art experience is necessary for any Soulistry Retreat or Workshop, whether on its own or in the context of a Conference.

A Spirituality of Play
Mime, music, creative spirituality journaling, movement, laughter and silence are interwoven in the creation of a personal clown as a spirituality of play is nurtured.

Awakening the Creative Spirit
As the 'ordinary' is transformed into the sacred, artistic soul-space is created, creativity is re-awakened, playful nature is released and spirituality is enriched in new ways.

Heartful Spirit
Spirit captures heart and mind as joy and creativity-within are discovered while working with a spiritual advisor, published author and Creative Spirituality Artist who encourages that intangible soul-essence of life in a variety of artistic experiences.

Creative Spirituality
Through Creative Spirituality Journaling, Photo Meditations and Soulistry Journal Prompts, discover how words can breathe life into art and how art and breathe life into words. In a quiet and sacred experience of artistic reflection, renewal and creativity, 'sight' becomes 'insight' and a unique way of uncovering the invisible presence of the holy in the visible world and within is discovered.

Paper Marbling Mystery

Explore the child-within and play with saran wrap, shaving cream, felt markers, colored inks, water, pastel chalks in new ways as beautiful one-of-a-kind marbled paper is created.

Mothers and Daughters: Creative Awakening

Through exploration of a fun, easy art technique and group discussion, mothers and daughters ignite their creative nature as their relationship is strengthened.

Opening to Mystery

Discover how Contemplative Photography (both art form and meditative resource) can be a way to connect with Mystery as enchantment, wonder and moments of intimate connection with the Creator are experienced.

Seeing ... With New Eyes

Church leaders learn how to see through the eyes of others and make gentle changes so that their church is perceived to be a more welcoming and inviting spiritual home by visitors and newcomers in this interactive and innovative workshop.

Sacred Death ... Holy Grief

In a safe, gentle and respectful setting, participants consider death and grieving as a natural part of life that is both sacred and holy.

For more information: soulistry@gmail.com
www.soulistry.com
http://www.soulistry.com/workshops

who am i?

familial roles identify
mother, wife
daughter, sister
aunt, cousin

occupational roles define
educator, consultant
broadcaster, journalist

vocational roles name
creative spirituality artist
spiritual director, priest
friend, writer
child of God

playful roles define
puppeteer, clown
flautist, blogger

who am i?
am i one person today
and tomorrow another
am i all, all at once
interwoven

who am i?
i'm me
evolving, unfolding, creating
discovering and re-discovering
the essence of the spirit within

© june mack maffin   www.soulistry.com

Circle Books

Circle is a symbol of infinity and unity. It's part of a growing list of imprints, including o-books.net and zero-books.net.

Circle Books aims to publish books in Christian spirituality that are fresh, accessible, and stimulating.

Our books are available in all good English language bookstores worldwide. If you can't find the book on the shelves, then ask your bookstore to order it for you, quoting the ISBN and title. Or, you can order online—all major online retail sites carry our titles.

To see our list of titles, please view www.Circle-Books.com, growing by 80 titles per year.

Authors can learn more about our proposal process by going to our website and clicking on Your Company > Submissions.

We define Christian spirituality as the relationship between the self and its sense of the transcendent or sacred, which issues in literary and artistic expression, community, social activism, and practices. A wide range of disciplines within the field of religious studies can be called upon, including history, narrative studies, philosophy, theology, sociology, and psychology. Interfaith in approach, Circle Books fosters creative dialogue with non-Christian traditions.

And tune into MySpiritRadio.com for our book review radio show, hosted by June-Elleni Laine, where you can listen to authors discussing their books.

MySpiritRadio